New Ways in Teaching Culture

Alvino E. Fantini, Editor

New Ways in TESOL Series II
Innovative Classroom Techniques
Jack C. Richards, Series Editor

Teachers of English to Speakers of Other Languages, Inc.

Typeset in Garamond Book and Tiffany Demi
by Capitol Communication Systems, Inc., Crofton, Maryland USA
and printed by
Pantagraph Printing, Bloomington, Illinois USA

Teachers of English to Speakers of Other Languages, Inc. (TESOL)
1600 Cameron Street, Suite 300
Alexandria, VA 22314 USA
Tel 703-836-0774 • Fax 703-836-7864 • e-mail: publ@tesol.edu • http://www.tesol.edu

Director of Communications and Marketing: Helen Kornblum
Managing Editor: Marilyn Kupetz
Cover Design: Ann Kammerer

TESOL thanks Barbara Jacobson, the staff, and the students at Northern Virginia Community College, Alexandria, Virginia, for their assistance and participation.

ISBN 0-939-791-70-6
Library of Congress Catalogue No. 96-061906

Contents

Part III: Activities for Sociolinguistic Exploration

Part IV: Activities for Culture Exploration

Part V: Activities for Intercultural Exploration

A Selective and Annotated Bibliography

Acknowledgments

A special volume of this sort required an extensive search to find individuals actively engaged in teaching culture and intercultural dimensions as part of their language classes. This meant numerous "calls for papers" among TESOL's international membership and beyond. A fertile place to find such individuals was the rapidly growing and kindred professional society known as SIETAR International (the Society for Intercultural Education, Training, and Research). Although its members are fully engaged in cross-cultural work, they are not exclusively language teachers and represent a wide variety of disciplines. Nonetheless, a "call" to SIETAR members yielded numerous submissions in addition to articles for the introductory section, which presents a conceptual backdrop for the activities that follow. Indeed, the focus of this volume requires the experiences of both language educators and interculturalists in its attempt to bridge the interests of both groups toward a common cause—the development of intercultural communicative competence. Needless to say, the number of individuals who responded was significant, and for this, I am grateful.

There are also individuals who merit special recognition. I would like to acknowledge first of all New Ways Series Editor Jack C. Richards, who approved this volume on teaching culture as well as Managing Editor Marilyn Kupetz, who provided guidance throughout the project. In addition, I would like to recognize individuals who made special contributions. I begin with Carolyn Ryffel, who was always ready to give an extra measure of help. Carolyn not only wrote an article for the introductory section but contributed a major part of the annotated bibliography. I express gratitude as well to two individuals who are well known to TESOL and SIETAR members: Ned Seelye and Milton Bennett, both of whom added their thoughts and talents to the conceptual background section. I thank Patricia Young, my graduate assistant in 1996, who helped to input documents and to provide support in so many other ways; Jim Davidson, a part-time assistant in 1995, who was a whiz with the computer and is now teaching EFL in Korea; and Shirley Capron, research librarian at the School for International Training, who tracked down references and various other details to ensure accuracy in this work. Last but not least, I am certainly indebted to the more than 50 contributors who responded to my calls and who are duly cited in the table of contents as well as at the end of each of the activities presented.

Foreword

Although the fields of language education and intercultural communication have both made important strides during the past quarter of a century, they have often wandered alone, along separate paths. This separation is evidenced in educational approaches to the teaching of foreign and second languages that do not explicitly and consistently incorporate culture/intercultural dimensions, in the dearth of university courses in intercultural communication within language teacher education programs—in fact, "only one third of programs offer a course in culture," according to Reid (1995/1996, p. 3)—and in the existence of separate professional societies for language teachers and those engaged in intercultural work.

Whereas language educators commonly express interest in culture as part of the language experience, they often treat culture as supplemental or incidental to the real task; interculturalists, conversely, interested in general intercultural communication, often fail to address how communication is mediated through a specific language. Moreover, language educators who demonstrate interest in "culture" often ignore "intercultural" concerns—that is, the contrasts between target and native languages and cultures and the dynamic tension between them. The general result is separate bodies of knowledge, separate gurus, separate fields.

Yet anyone who has worked in both areas quickly recognizes the need for holistic approaches when preparing individuals for intercultural experiences, approaches that combine the development of language proficiency with the related competencies needed for the challenges posed by intercultural contact and entry. Although the intercultural field is itself interdisciplinary, sometimes multidisciplinary, and occasionally transdisciplinary in perspective, language and language issues are normally left to language teachers. Language teachers, on the other hand, are often unaware of developments in the intercultural field. There is a need, then, to reconceptualize both fields—language education and intercultural communication—to grasp better the whole, the components, and their interconnectedness, and to create training and education designs that include language and intercultural communication activities.

Happily, we are already witnessing dramatic changes. Whereas ESOL teachers may have always been more concerned with practical aspects of communicating, interest is clearly picking up among those in the foreign language profession as well. In November 1995, at its annual convention, the American Council on the Teaching of Foreign Languages (ACTFL) presented the results of a 3-year project, conducted in collaboration with various other language societies, in the form of *The National Standards in Foreign Education*. Among the five goal areas, the need for both learning about cultures and comparing them is clearly and explicitly cited—direct references to the inclusion of little "c" culture (in addition to traditional culture with a capital "C") and to intercultural exploration. Similarly, TESOL published *Promising Futures: ESL Standards for Pre-K-12 Students* (1996), citing as its third goal: "To use English in socially and culturally appropriate ways" (p. 17). The narrative under the goal adds, "In order to work and live amid diversity, students need to be able to understand and appreciate people who are different and communicate effectively with them. Communicating effectively also means having the ability to interact in multiple social settings" (p. 17). The stage is indeed set for good things to follow.

I hope that this volume will further the process. For this reason, I envisioned it as a forum for compiling ideas among those actively exploring the nexus between language, culture, and world view, while encouraging them to share their work with the general readership of the TESOL New Ways series. I hope the articles and activities that follow will contribute to our field's ongoing development and to the recognition that language, culture, and intercultural work belong together.

References and Further Reading

ACTFL. (1995). *The national standards in foreign education.* New York: Author.

Reid, J. (1995/1996, December/January). President's message: Let's put the "T" back in TESL/TEFL programs. *TESOL Matters,* p. 3.

TESOL. (1996). *Promising futures: ESL standards for pre-K-12 students.* Alexandria, VA: Author.

Overview

This volume of the New Ways Series focuses on new ways of teaching cultural and intercultural dimensions of ESOL. The first section presents theoretical concepts about our understanding of language, culture, and world view, suggesting implications and applications for teaching English as either a second or foreign language (ESL or EFL). Parts II–V are entirely devoted to classroom activities that illustrate innovative ways of including culture and intercultural exploration as an integral part of the language experience. The final part contains a selected and annotated bibliography of works to encourage readers to go beyond the scope of this book and to further their work.

Introductory Articles

I chose the five introductory articles to offer a theoretical and conceptual framework for why and how to include culture and intercultural dimensions when teaching ESOL. In the first article, "Language: Its Cultural and Intercultural Dimensions, " I try to bridge the world of language education and intercultural communications and detail a rationale for exploring new ways in teaching culture. The second article, by Milton Bennett, reinforces this rationale and cautions against becoming a "fluent fool"—one who gains language proficiency but not also intercultural savvy and is therefore at risk when interacting with members of the target culture. H. Ned Seelye follows with an essay proposing six goals toward achieving intercultural communicative competence. Next, Carolyn Ryffel provides some important thoughts about how to structure and conduct the exercises and activities in this book to ensure their effectiveness. I present two final items in this part: a "Process Approach" framework to aid in choosing and using the activities that follow and an excerpt from a teacher development instrument that spells out some professional competencies in culture/intercultural areas for the language teacher.

Activities

The next four sections contain 50 classroom activities submitted by contributors from around the world. These are grouped into four areas: activities to explore the nexus between language and culture, activities for sociolinguistic exploration, activities for culture exploration, and, finally, those for intercultural exploration. These activities should be of immediate use to the classroom teacher, containing specific details about aims, preparation, procedures, and the like.

Annotated Bibliography

An annotated bibliography of selected works completes the volume. Its aim is to provide the reader with a source of many related works beyond the scope of this treatment. The references are grouped into six sections, with works on

- intercultural theory
- intercultural competence
- cultural differences affecting foreign language learning
- ways of integrating culture
- cross-cultural activities
- specific cultures and countries

Index

This index will help you select activities to suit your purposes.

I hope the reader will find these varied and interesting contributions of use in helping learners to become both language proficient and interculturally competent.

Alvino E. Fantini
School for International Training
Brattleboro, Vermont United States

Part I: Introductory Articles—
Conceptual Background for Activities

From left to right Kimbunda Mwasa Jolie, Sora Han, and Catering Ramos at Northern Virginia Community College, Alexandria, Virginia USA.

Language: Its Cultural and Intercultural Dimensions*

Alvino E. Fantini

The Goal of This Special Volume

If educators in the language and intercultural fields had a shared goal, it would certainly be the development of intercultural communicative competence (ICC, or intercultural competence for short). A special issue of the *International Journal of Intercultural Relations (IJIR)* (Martin, 1989) and a more recent endeavor (Wiseman & Koester, 1993) attempted to gather studies on just this topic. Although many aspects of ICC competence are presented, three principal themes emerge:

1. the ability to establish relations
2. the ability to communicate with minimal loss or distortion
3. the ability to achieve or attain a level of compliance among those involved

Stated this way, these abilities are desirable, if not altogether necessary, for everyone everywhere. Not only are these aspects part of "intercultural relations," they are also germane to "interpersonal relations." What complicates matters at the intercultural level, however, is that when interacting with individuals across cultures, we share fewer and fewer commonalities while other variables increase:

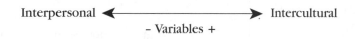

Interpersonal ⟷ Intercultural
– Variables +

---

*Adapted from "Language, Culture and World View: Exploring the Nexus," by Alvino E. Fantini, 1995, *International Journal of Intercultural Relations, 19*, pp. 143–153. Printed with permission from Elsevier Science Ltd.

Most notable are the variables that are presented by differences in languages, cultures, and world views that mediate our interaction. For this reason, both language educators and interculturalists share a role in expanding and developing native competence into intercultural competence for use in a wider arena.

A goal of intercultural competence, then, requires insights drawn from both language and intercultural areas. With rare exception (see Ting-Toomey & Korzenny, 1989), however, interculturalists often overlook (or leave to language teachers) the task of developing language competence, just as language teachers overlook (or leave to interculturalists) the task of developing intercultural abilities. This, despite wide acknowledgment that language and culture are dimensions of each other, interrelated and inseparable. Language, in fact, both reflects and affects one's world view, serving as a sort of road map to how one perceives, interprets and thinks about, and expresses one's views of the world. This intertwining invites a fresh look at how we conceptualize what is meant by world view, its components, and their interrelationships; and how language and culture mediate (inter)cultural processes.

Stated this way, ICC is clearly also a goal of several other kindred groups. It is the ardent concern of those laboring in bilingual education, multicultural education, ethnic heritage and ethnic revival education, foreign and second language education, and international and global education. All strive to develop the awareness, attitudes, skills, and knowledge (A+ASK) that take one beyond one's native paradigm while grappling with another that is intrinsically and provocatively different.

Linguistics and the Intercultural Field

Because linguistics predates the intercultural field, it has had many more years to develop concepts about language and language use, concepts that can be helpful in informing language educators and interculturalists about their own work. Surprisingly, too few interculturalists have linguistics as part of their formation; more surprising still is to find interculturalists—and some ESOL language educators—without proficiency in a second language. More than the actual attainment of proficiency is the fact that without a second language experience, they have not grappled with the most fundamental paradigm of all—language, and the benefits that derive from this process. For all of the research and concepts *about* other cultures and world views, the monolingual ESOL teacher or interculturalist engages mostly in intellectualized endeavors when concepts are not also accompanied by *direct* experiences of other cultures and languages. Without an alternative form of communication, we are constrained to continue perception, conceptualization, formulation, and expression of our thoughts from a single vantage point. Despite our ability to discuss ad infinitum intercultural concepts in our own tongue, our experiences remain vicarious and intellectualized, lacking multiple perspectives, which Fishman (1976) characterized as ". . . monocular vision . . . which can lead to narrow smugness and a smug narrowness."

Because language is considerably more tangible and easier to document than culture, linguists are often better able to analyze and understand their data. Yet, much of what is gleaned from a linguistic perspective about languages informs our understanding of culture. Because language reflects and affects culture, and because both languages and cultures are human inventions, it is not surprising this should be so. A linguistic concept illustrating this point and widely used in the intercultural field (cf., Gudykunst & Nishida, 1989) is the notion of *etic* and *emic* perspectives (seeing from the outside as a foreigner vs. seeing from the inside as a native). The utility of linguistic insight to intercultural thought is perhaps best supported in the works of Edward Hall and may account for his proposition that "culture *is* communication" (Hall, 1973, p. 97) just as we might add that, "communication *is* culture."

When analyzed further, the depth of this simple comment is even more apparent. It is often said that the anthropoid is transformed into a human being through language acquisition. Language, that is, our total communicative ability, allows us to develop "human" qualities by learning from vicarious and symbolic (as well as direct) experiences, to help formulate our thoughts, and to convey them to someone else. Without language, none of this is possible. Put another way, communicative ability allows culture development through interaction and communication with other individuals. Language serves as the construct that aids cultural development.

Studies of wolf and feral children, as well as those of older adults raised in isolation, attest to the incredible constraints that lack of any communication system exerts on their development as human beings (e.g., Brown, 1958; Curtiss, 1977; Lane, 1976; Rymer, 1993; Schaller, 1991). But for those undergoing "normal" development, language affects and reflects culture just as culture affects and reflects what is encoded in language. Although language and culture do not perfectly mirror each other, a dynamic tension nonetheless exists between the two. Whorf and Piaget observed such influences, although each emphasized a different starting point (Piaget in Spencer Pulaski, 1971; Steinfatt, 1989; Whorf, 1956).

A Language-Culture Paradigm

A linguistic construct that depicts how language exteriorizes one's perceptions of the world (as it helps in turn to develop one's internalized view) is the following input-output framework:

How Language Exteriorizes Perceptions

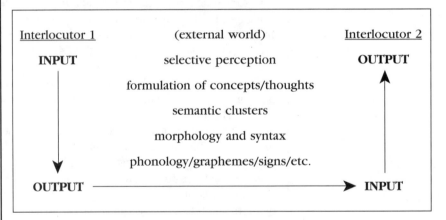

Interlocutor 1	(external world)	Interlocutor 2
INPUT	selective perception	**OUTPUT**
	formulation of concepts/thoughts	
	semantic clusters	
	morphology and syntax	
	phonology/graphemes/signs/etc.	
OUTPUT ——————————————→		**INPUT**

To elaborate further on this model, we find ourselves in a given context (external world). However, each individual (in accordance with one's language, culture, and experiences) selectively attends to (i.e., perceives) certain aspects of that context. Perceptions (apprehended through the various senses) are formulated into concepts or thoughts, essentially a mental process. However, communication of one's thoughts to another person requires reformulation of thought into tangible manifestations (in accordance with one's available language systems). Thoughts are "reinterpreted" while grouped by semantic features (which eventually become words or signs) when shaped (i.e., given morphological form) and ordered sequentially (because language can only be conveyed linearly; that is, one word placed after another in accordance with the available syntactic system), couched within existing symbols (sounds, script, gestures, and so forth), and then expressed physically. The mental aspect of this process is what Noam Chomsky termed *competence*, while the physical expression is one's *performance* (corresponding to deep and surface structures).

Whereas one gathers input through perception, one's expression through tangible symbols provides the output. Input and output are interconnected within each speaker through mental processes that are mediated at both deep and surface levels by the particular language of the speaker. Language symbols, however, provide the "substance" that allows thought to be exteriorized.

Assuming two interlocutors share a similar language-culture background, output from the first provides comprehensible input for the second. In this way, they can alternately reverse the process during dialogue, at times moving from perception to thought to expression (from input to output); and at others, receiving someone else's symbolic output as input. The process is then reversed to create a facsimile of the other's mental representations (providing another way of experiencing and "knowing"). However, this process of converting perception to thought, and thought to language, necessarily requires breaking down and fragmenting holistic experience in accordance with the word categories available in one's own tongue because each language system consists of discrete units, conveyed one symbol at a time.

In this way, language serves as a primary classificatory system, segmenting and fragmenting our notions about the world while also grouping and combining word categories, ranging from wider classifications to narrower specifications based on semantic criteria that are clustered and form their meaning. Moreover, words cohere in hierarchies (from general to specific) with other words sharing many of the same semantic features (Anglin, 1970, 1995), whereas hierarchies mesh into hetararchies (a hierarchy of hierarchies). As we learn our native tongue, we learn to generalize and specify about the things of the world as we encode concepts into the words of language, just as the words of language in turn lead us to concepts.

More intriguing still is to recognize that each language-culture establishes its own hetararchy. Hall (1973) says as much when he points out that "there is no necessary connection between these symbolizations and what occurred. Talking is a highly selective process . . . highlighting some things at the expense of some other things" (pp. 97–98). He alludes, of course, to language-thought connections as arbitrary convention or conventionalized arbitrariness, a concept advanced a century ago by Saussure (1961). Yet, once the relationship is established, it remains rather fixed. This relationship between experience, thought, and expression, then, speaks to how language and culture mediate world view, serving as our most fundamental paradigm.

Language Unawareness

Why is it then that we take language for granted, unaware that our native tongue is not merely a "neutral" communication system, but a pervasive medium that directly influences every aspect of our lives? It may be because we seldom need to reflect on our use of language; it has been there for as long as we can remember. And therein lies the power of a different cultural experience. While providing a chance to learn about another way of life, it provokes even more questions about one's own language, culture, and world view.

By 5 years of age, children have already become effective members of their culture, displaying amazing language ability. They use this ability to explore, to learn, to communicate, and to formulate simple and sometimes very profound questions. Unaware of their own accomplishments—mastery of complex patterns of sounds (or signs), forms, and syntax—children acquire their native tongue unthinkingly, its acquisition incidental to their need to perform all that they do with language (Fantini, 1985).

Moreover, language is species-specific. Animals do not acquire language; only humans do. All human children everywhere develop speech—with ease, untutored, and in similar stages. Yet, the language paradigm is our most basic metaphor because word creations substitute for the thing signified. As we master words, we often fail to distinguish between verbal symbols and the reality for which they stand. But words can only evoke conceptually what is meant, thereby providing vicarious mental experiences for speaker and hearer. Once acquired, words have the power to mediate what we think, say, and do. Through language, we have the power to recreate events experienced, but also to talk of things we "know" only indirectly through symbols. Language aids (and sometimes limits) imagination, fantasy, the make-believe. Real or imagined, language can bring into existence even that which may not exist at all. And once experienced, directly or indirectly, language becomes a repository for our collective human memory—or at least for the memory of those who share the same tongue—generation after generation.

Language—A Two-Edged Sword

Language is a double-edged sword: Language communicates, but it also excommunicates. That is, it includes only those who share the system; others are excluded. Likewise, language both liberates and constrains. Our ability to symbolize, for example, allows us to move freely, albeit conceptually, through time and space. We can recall and tell of things past, or project into the future, merely by uttering words. So great is our faith in words that we can viscerally experience the "reality" of something we never experienced directly at all, whether in the past or the future. Yet, there is no way to retrieve the past nor ensure the future; we can only symbolize about them while we remain always only in the present moment and space.

Just as language conveys thoughts and experiences, it can also constrain and contradict them. Through language we learn, for example, that things are not always what they seem. In fact, much of what we learn and "know" we really do not "know" at all—that is, directly. Knowledge is tremendously augmented through language use. Much of schooling and other learning in life is accomplished through language, expanding the limits of what we can know through direct experience alone. Language permits contemplating the impossible and exploring the unfathomable. We talk about concepts as difficult and as abstract as "death," for example, which we can never know directly, at least not in life. It is difficult to imagine what life might be like without our human ability to symbolize, just as it is difficult to imagine how we might think or know differently if we spoke a language other than our native tongue, or in addition to it.

Language as Communicative Competence

By giving tangible expression to thought, language enables communication with others. Although speech signals are often part of communicative ability, there are other forms as well—written symbols, signed language, and other means. Whichever we use, these are usually combined, forming several interrelated systems:

- a linguistic component (sounds, signs and/or graphemes, forms, and grammar of language)
- a paralinguistic component (tone, pitch, volume, speed, and affective aspects)
- an extralinguistic component (nonverbal aspects such as gestures, movements, grimaces)
- when context is considered, a sociolinguistic dimension (a repertoire of styles, each appropriate for different situations)

All are mastered in overlapping stages as part of one's native competence. Understanding these multiple dimensions and their interrelatedness elucidates what is involved when developing competence in a second or third system.

During the past quarter of a century, the notion of *communicative competence* has increasingly commanded the attention of language teachers and interculturalists alike. For language teachers, it suggests that teaching "language" means more than the linguistic (i.e., grammar) component alone. In practice, however, linguistic considerations often continue to preempt the major portion of time in classroom teaching. For interculturalists, on the other hand, a common approach to communicative competence includes culture-specific ethnographic studies based on the work of Hymes' (1972) framework (cf. Carbaugh, 1990); as well as attempts to extend this sociolinguistic framework to intercultural interaction (cf. Collier, 1989). In these endeavors, however, the language component is often superseded by a focus on the communicative rules of interaction.

The term, nonetheless, signifies the whole and helps remind us about all aspects of the communication process. In a similar vein, language and culture may also require a broader label, a superordinate term that connotes and ensures their inseparability. The term *linguaculture* has served this purpose in my own work; and recently, another writer proposed the word *languaculture* (Agar, 1994). Both reflect attempts to link the inextricable phenomena of language and culture conceptually and operationally.

Language and World View

Language, that is, communicative competence (our expanded definition of language), reflects and reinforces a particular view we hold of the world. In linguistic terms, the influence of language on culture and world view is called *language determinism and relativity*; that is, the language we acquire influences the way we construct our model of the world (hence, determinism). And if this is so, other languages convey differing visions of that same world (relativity). This long debated theory, known as the Sapir-Whorfian hypothesis, raises intriguing issues related to cross-cultural effectiveness (Steinfatt, 1989; Whorf, 1956). To this, Hall (1976) adds: "Man is the model-making organism par excellence .... grammars and writing systems are models of language," while cautioning that "all models are incomplete. By definition, they are abstractions and leave things out" (pp. 10–11).

How effectively and appropriately can an individual behave in an intercultural context with—or without—ability in the target language? Notions of "effectiveness" and "appropriateness" suggest two views of the issue. Whereas effectiveness is often a judgment from one's own perspective, appropriateness is based on judgments made from the host's perspective. Although communication across cultures may occur in one's own language (especially where English or another dominant language is involved), there is a qualitative difference between communicating in one's own language and in the language of one's hosts. Whichever the case, second language (L2) proficiency is critical to functioning effectively and appropriately in cross-cultural situations, plus the added benefit that exposure to a second linguaculture (LC2) affords an opportunity to develop a different or, at least, an expanded vision of the world. Needless to say, developing a LC3 or LC4 is even better in that it demands reconfiguring polarizations that sometimes occur in the mind of bilingual-bicultural individuals.

The following illustration delineates how components of each linguaculture form a cohesive world view and how world views differ from each other:

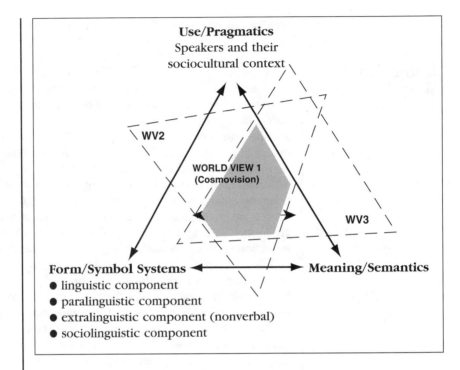

These interrelated components form the basis for each world view construct, but because they vary in detail from culture to culture, they result in a differing realization of the world for each group of speakers. This explains why developing a LC2 (i.e., becoming bilingual and bicultural) involves more than mastery of language as tool (the surface features), but grasping how the components themselves are reconfigured. The result is a transformation that affects one's view of the world, changing and expanding it. Although each world view differs (in particular aspects), the shaded areas where triangles overlap suggest aspects shared by all human beings (universals). Despite the marvelous diversity and creativity across the linguacultures of the world, the overlap hints at the existence of universals across all, an aspect that researchers have begun to investigate more seriously in recent years. These universals may result from our common humanity, ensured by similar biological and physical possibilities and constraints.

Success with our native linguaculture (LC1), unfortunately, does not always ensure equal success with a LC2. In fact, an individual's LC1 is often the biggest impediment to acquiring a second. Establishment of one paradigm, especially in adult learners, commonly prevents developing a second, at least not without serious question, deep scrutiny, and reflection, unlike in young children raised bilingually and biculturally (Fantini, 1985). For older individuals, developing intercultural competence comes with a cost, with challenges, shocks, and reservations; and as anyone who has undergone an intercultural experience knows, the choices we make bear consequences, for ourselves and for those with whom we interact (Adler, 1976).

The Potential— Transcending

Developing intercultural competence for ourselves and for others is a shared challenge—for language educators and interculturalists alike—but its attainment promises rewards. Intercultural competence offers the possibility of transcending the limitations of one's singular world view. "If you want to know about water, don't ask a goldfish" is a frequent quote heard among interculturalists. Those who have never experienced another culture nor labored to communicate through a second language, like the goldfish, are often unaware of the milieu in which they have always existed.

Contact with other world views can result in a shift of perspective, along with a concomitant appreciation for the diversity and richness of human beings. This paradigm shift is the kind that one writer portrayed as an historic revolution, one that occurs in the head and the mind, as personal transformation and "change from the inside out" (Ferguson, 1980, pp. 17-20).

As language educators, we may indeed have a significant role in that revolution. A concern with cross-cultural effectiveness and appropriateness—coupled with second or foreign language development—will, I hope, lead beyond tolerance and understanding to a genuine appreciation of others. For this to happen, we need to develop the awareness, attitudes, skills, and knowledge that will make us better participants on a local and global level, able to understand and to empathize with others in new ways. Exposure to more than one language, culture, and world view, in a positive context, offers such a promise.

References

Adler, P. S. (1976). Beyond culture identity. In L. A. Samovar & R. E. Porter (Eds.), *Intercultural communication* (2nd ed., pp. 362–380). Belmont, CA: Wadsworth.

Agar, M. (1994). The intercultural frame. *International Journal of Intercultural Relations, 18,* 221–237.

Anglin, J. M. (1970). *The growth of word meaning*. Cambridge, MA: MIT Press.

Anglin, J. M. (1995). Classifying the world through language. *The International Journal of Intercultural Relations, 19,* 161–181.

Brown, R. (1958). *Words and things*. New York: The Free Press.

Carbaugh, D. (Ed.). (1990). *Cultural communication and intercultural contact*. Hillsdale, NJ: Lawrence Erlbaum.

Collier, M. J. (1989). Cultural and intercultural communication competence. *International Journal of Intercultural Relations, 13,* 287–302.

Curtiss, S. (1977). *Genie: A psycholinguistic study of a modern-day "wild child."* New York: Academic Press.

Fantini, A. E. (1985). *Language acquisition of a bilingual child*. Clevedon, England: Multilingual Matters; also (1982) *La acquisición del lenguaje en un niño bilingüe*. Barcelona, Spain: Editorial Herder.

Fantini, A. E. (Ed.). (1995). Special issue: Language, culture and world view. *International Journal of Intercultural Relations, 19*(2).

Ferguson, M. (1980). *The Aquarian conspiracy*. Los Angeles: J. P. Tarcher.

Fishman, J. (1976). *Bilingual education: An international sociological perspective*. Recorded keynote address, 5th International Bilingual Education Conference, San Antonio, TX.

Gudykunst, W. B., & Nishida, T. (1989). Theoretical perspectives for studying intercultural communication. In M. K. Asante & W. S. Gudykunst (Eds.), *Handbook of international and intercultural communication* (pp. 17–46). Newbury Park, CA: Sage.

Hall, E. T. (1973). *The silent language*. New York: Doubleday.

Hall, E. T. (1976). *Beyond culture*. New York: Doubleday.

Hymes, D. (1972). Models of the interaction of language and social life. In J. Gumperz & D. Hymes (Eds.), *Directions in sociolinguistics: The ethnography of communication* (pp. 1–72). New York: Holt, Rinehart & Winston.

Lane, H. (1976). *The wild boy of Aveyron.* Cambridge, MA: Harvard University Press.

Martin, J. (Guest Ed.). (1989). Special issue: Intercultural communication competence. *International Journal of Intercultural Relations, 13*(3).

Rymer, R. (1993). *Genie: An abused child's flight from silence.* New York: HarperCollins.

Saussure, F. de (1961). *Curso de lingüística general.* Buenos Aires, Argentina: Editorial Losada.

Schaller, S. (1991). *A man without words.* New York: Summit Books.

Spencer Pulaski, M. A. (1971). *Understanding Piaget.* New York: Harper & Row.

Steinfatt, T. M. (1989). Linguistic relativity: Toward a broader view. In S. Ting-Toomey & F. Korzenny (Eds.), *Language, communication and culture: Current directions* (pp. 35–78). Newbury Park, CA: Sage.

Ting-Toomey, S., & Korzenny, F. (Eds.). (1989). *Language, communication and culture: Current directions.* Newbury Park, CA: Sage.

Whorf, B. L. (1956). *Language, thought and reality.* Cambridge, MA: MIT Press.

Wiseman, R. L., & Koester, J. (Eds.). (1993). *Intercultural communication competence.* Newbury Park, CA: Sage.

How Not to Be a Fluent Fool: Understanding the Cultural Dimension of Language*

Milton J. Bennett

Many students (and some teachers) view language only as a communication tool—a method humans use to indicate the objects and ideas of their physical and social world. In this view, languages are sets of words tied together by rules, and learning a foreign or second language is the simple (but tedious) process of substituting words and rules to get the same meaning with a different tool.

This kind of thinking can lead to becoming a "fluent fool." A fluent fool is someone who speaks a foreign language well but doesn't understand the social or philosophical content of that language. Such people are likely to get into all sorts of trouble because both they themselves and others overestimate their ability. They may be invited into complicated social situations where they cannot understand the events deeply enough to avoid giving or taking offense. Eventually, fluent fools may develop negative opinions of the native speakers whose language they understand but whose basic beliefs and values continue to elude them.

To avoid becoming a fluent fool, we need to understand more completely the cultural dimension of language. Language does serve as a tool for communication, but in addition it is a "system of representation" for perception and thinking. This function of language provides us with verbal categories and prototypes that guide our formation of concepts and categorization of objects; it directs how we experience reality.

Language and Experience

A memorable statement of language representing experience was made by Whorf (1956):

> We dissect nature along lines laid down by our native languages. The categories and types that we isolate from the world of phenomena we do not find there because they stare every observer in the face; on the contrary, the world is represented in a kaleidoscopic flux of impressions which has been organized in our minds—and this means largely by the linguistic systems in our minds. (p. 213)

In this statement, Whorf advances what has come to be called the "strong form" of the Whorf hypothesis: Language largely determines the way in which we understand our reality. In other writings, Whorf takes the position that language, thought, and perception are interrelated, a position called the "weak hypothesis."

In either case of the Whorf hypothesis, the implication for language teachers is clear: Language teaching is also reality teaching. The instruction that foreign and second language teachers provide in linguistic construction necessarily includes guidelines on how to experience reality in a different way.

I was an ESOL instructor in the Micronesian islands of Truk when I first noticed this other dimension of language teaching. My primary school class was doing well in substituting color names in the sentence:"I see a _____ ball" in response to pictures of different colored balls. But when I showed them the blue ball, the pattern became garbled. The same thing happened when I showed the green ball. The students could pronounce the words, but they couldn't recognize the difference between these two colors. Further investigation revealed that native speakers of Trukese have only one word, *araw*, to refer to both blue and green colors. *Araw* is the response to either question, "What color is the sea?" or "What color is the grass?" While teaching these students English, I was also teaching them how to experience something (the difference between blue and green) that they did not experience using their own language. (For research on the topic of naming colors, see Kay & Kempton, 1984.)

Language and the Classification of Objects

Another example of how various languages direct different experiences of reality is found in how objects and space are represented. American English has only one way to count things (one, two, three, etc.), whereas Japanese and Trukese each have many different counting systems. In part, these systems classify the physical appearance of objects. For instance, in Trukese one (long) thing is counted with different words from one (flat) thing or one (round) thing. We could imagine that the experience of objects in general is much richer in cultures where language devotes attention to subtle differences in shape. Indeed, Japanese aesthetic appreciation of objects also seems more elaborate than that of Americans, whose English language lacks linguistic structures to represent shapes in its counting system.

In addition, both Japanese and Trukese count people with a set of words different from all others used for objects. We might speculate that research on human beings that quantifies behavior "objectively," so common in Western cultures, would not arise as easily in cultures where people were counted distinctly.

In American English, things can be either *here* or *there*, with a colloquial attempt to place them further out *over there*. In the Trukese language, references to objects and people must be accompanied by a location marker that specifies their position relative to both the speaker and the listener. A pen, for instance, must be called *this* (close to me but away from you) pen, *this* (midway between us) pen, *that* (far away from both of us but in sight (pen), or *that* (out of sight of both of us) pen. Again, we may assume that Trukese people experience "richer" space than do Americans, whose language does not provide as many spatial boundary markers and for whom space is therefore more abstract.

Language in Social Relations

The experimental evidence available clearly supports a Whorf effect in social perception. People's percepts of social events and situations, social relations, roles, and even their own behavior are distinctively in keeping with the different conceptual structures of their languages (Fisher, 1972, p. 99).

Perhaps the simplest and best known examples are linguistic differences in status markers. Thai, Japanese, and various other Asian languages have elaborate systems of second person singular (*you*) words that indicate the status of the speaker relative to the listener. In Thai, there are also variable forms of *I* to indicate relative status. Thus, *I* (relatively lower in status) may be speaking to *you* (somewhat higher in status) or to *you* (much higher in status), using a different form of *I* and *you* in each case. It seems apparent that cultures with languages that demand recognition of relative status in every direct address will encourage more acute experience of status difference than does American culture, where English provides only one form of *you*. European cultures, most of whose languages have two forms of *you,* indicating both status distinctions and familiarity, may represent the middle range of this dimension. Europeans are more overtly attentive to status than are Americans, but Europeans are no match for Asians in this regard.

Language Structure as a Model for Thinking

Thus far we have used semantic examples to examine the influence of language on thought. To complete the case for the Whorf effect, we should briefly consider the impact of the syntactic structure of language on thinking. Two aspects of linguistics, forms of verb tense and subject/predicate structure, yield evidence of cultural representation in thought.

The Trukese language lacks an elaborate future tense, and Trukese people may be observed living more in the present than planning for the future. For instance, arrangements for future events such as meetings or boat trips are always tentative, when they are made at all. It may be an overstatement to say that the lack of a future tense dictates present-orientation, but Whorf (1956) made a similar observation about the Hopis, whose language also lacks a future tense. The Hopi people use statements of intentions to refer to future events; and Hopi behavior, like Trukese, displays qualities of present-orientation. Americans, using English with its far more developed future tense, aim toward the near future, stress planning, and project the future in making decisions.

Speakers of English are also forced by the subect-verb-object syntactic form to constantly represent causality. When there is a predicate in the language but no subject, the structure of English requires that the speaker assume one. The word *it* often suffices for the missing subject, as in, *It happened one night.* The implication is that "happenings" do not simply occur on their own (as they can in Japanese, for instance); there is something (*it*) behind them.

In its conception of action and events, English is an actor-action-result model, and tends to suggest that perception of this universe and what happens in it. The actor-action-result pattern is very useful for conceptualizing mechanics, business and much of science. It suggests the question "What caused that?" or "What effect will this have on the end result?" (Fisher, 1972, p. 120)

We can conclude that an imposing array of assumptions, values, and linguistic features of English predispose Americans to interpret events in the world as lineal chains of causes and effects. In contrast, other languages (such as Chinese) predispose their speakers toward perceiving complementary relationships.

Fluency Without Foolishness

To avoid turning out fluent fools, language teachers can be more deliberate in helping students learn to experience reality in a new way. Using a "culture-contrast" approach may be useful in this regard, including the following steps:

1. Inform students about how their native language is related to basic values, beliefs, thought patterns, and social action in their own cultures. This may be easier to do with Japanese students than with others because descriptions of Japanese culture already are couched in terms of linguistic concepts (e.g., *tatemai* or *wa*).
2. Compare native language-culture patterns to those of the new language-culture. Look especially for concepts and structures in the new language that do not exist in the native language because they provide keys to shifting experience along lines provided by the acquired language.
3. Assess achievement not just in terms of vocabulary and grammar but also in the pragmatic dimensions of culturally appropriate social judgment and decision making. Case studies or critical incidents accompanied by various possible actions can be useful in assessing a student's ability to shift his or her frame of reference toward that of the new language.

References and Further Reading

Fisher, G. (1972). *Public diplomacy and the behavioral sciences*. Bloomington: Indiana University Press.

Kay, P., & Kempton, W. (1984). What is the Sapir-Whorf hypothesis? *American Anthropologist, 86,* 65–79.

Stewart, E., & Bennett, M. (1991). *American cultural patterns* (rev. ed.). Yarmouth, ME: Intercultural Press.

Whorf, B. (1956). *Language, thought and reality* (J. B. Carroll, Ed.). New York: John Wiley & Sons.

Cultural Goals for Achieving Intercultural Communicative Competence*

H. Ned Seelye

Why Culture?

Human thought and behavior are mainly the consequence of three things: biochemically driven drives and predispositions (these are constant across cultures); the physical environment (these vary even within cultures); and the values and perspectives one shares with one's socializing group(s). (These latter, as operationalized in behavioral patterns, are mostly culture-specific.) The three influences are interactive.

The basic utility of culture as a theoretical construct is to focus attention on the influence that shared, in-group socialization exerts on thought and action. Individual, idiosyncratic behaviors also occur, but they too are filtered through, and shaped by, one's genetic inheritance, circumstance, and socialization. The *idea* of culture allows us to address the mind-boggling repercussions that human thought systems engender, from *abbatoirs* to *zamacuecas.* This idea or construct of culture helps us to see, and to categorize for small-bite consumption, a symphony of social conventions—what's prized, what's despised—that profoundly affect how we think and act.

Culturally driven behavior is learned behavior (as opposed to instinctual behavior), but not all learned behavior is of cultural origin. Learned behavior is principally cultural if it is information shared by the in-group, transmitted socially and historically, and systemic. Language behavior is a subset of cultural behavior.

Toward Consensus on the Parameters of a Culture Construct

As Bennett and Fantini argue in other sections of this book, it has become evident that the study of language cannot be divorced from the study of culture, and vice versa. The wherewithal to function in another cultural system requires both prowess in the language and knowledge of the culture.

Culture provides the software of the mind, without which most behavior would be random, unpredictable, and meaningless to other people. Culture is proscriptive; it tells us how to behave within our in-group. The shared rules passed down through the medium of culture enable individuals to relate to their place under the sun. When we look in on people "relating," we see them mixing action and speech. They do ingenious things to foreign words to incorporate them into their own idiom. They talk in nonstandard dialects within the same speech area. They talk one way to strangers and another way among themselves. They mix different languages in the same conversation. The words they use evoke cultural images of novel shapes and sizes. The way people speak indicates their sex, age, social class, and place of residence, and often conveys information concerning their religion, occupation, and interests.

There are many, many particular definitions of culture. My own definition: Culture is the systemic, rather arbitrary, more or less coherent, group-invented, and group-shared creed from the past that defines the shape of "reality," and assigns the sense and worth of things; it is modified by each generation and in response to adaptive pressures; it provides the code that tells people how to behave predictably and acceptably, the cipher that allows them to derive meaning from language and other symbols, the map that supplies the behavioral options for satisfying human needs. Don't take this definition too seriously, though; it is drawn in sand. The reader is invited to smooth it over and draw his or her own.

Rather than argue pointlessly and futilely about which one definition fits external reality best, it is more productive for us to ask which definition of culture is more useful to teachers of intercultural communicative competence. The resulting definition will be narrower than the ones used by many social scientists, but broader than the ones used by those who specialize in linguistics, literature, or the fine arts. It will probably focus on the communicable character of cultural information. Teachers of intercultural communication may not yet have an elegant definition of culture, but they are getting the idea that culture is a useful construct.

Devising Instructional Goals That Relate to the Cultural Context of Communication

Fantini, earlier in this book, discusses the pressing relevance of cultural context to communicative competence. In tailoring a language curriculum to suit the goal of facilitating intercultural communication, let us ask which attitudes and skills are critical to functioning in another culture. Four come immediately to mind.

First, ventures into intercultural territories require skill in learning new ways. Second, once there, it is crucial to establish rapport with people from the host culture. Third, we are pressed to learn how to make sense of the behavior of the host people, to see the systemic coherence in their thought and action. And fourth, it is critical to develop symbolic encoding devices, such as fluency in the language, that increase the probability of getting accurate meaning from language and nonlinguistic symbols alike.

Learning new ways is aided by a stark awareness that perceiving meaning signaled in another cultural setting requires recognizing the limits of our own "alien" and ethnocentric view of reality, and that stress often accompanies this budding awareness. Learning new ways also involves learning new things. That is why skill in locating and organizing information about the host culture is especially useful. A corollary skill is the ability to evaluate the strength of generalizations about a given culture, for all we hear and read is not well informed.

Rapport begins with enough interest in people from other cultures to go out of your way to talk to them. Rapport is abetted when you have learned information about their culture and country, including its geographic location, and can show your appreciation of their accomplishments and compassion for their difficulties.

Making sense of novel patterns of behavior is accomplished by understanding how the cultural system works to enable people to deal with basic physical and socializing needs such as hunger, love, vanity, and fear, and how role expectations and other social variants affect the way people speak and behave. This skill, like rapport, is a prerequisite to accurate communication.

Accurate intercultural communication is built on fluency in the target language, insight into what people are imaging when they speak, and the ability to decipher nonlinguistic symbols such as gestures and icons. Because people use language to aid and complement other behavioral purposes, language cannot be understood in isolation from the larger context of behavior—all of which is culturally filtered, and most of which is culturally originated.

How can an ESOL or foreign language teacher approach, at least in part, the task of developing student skill in those socially contextual areas that are the requisites of intercultural communicative competence? A first step is to identify appropriate instructional goals. Six examples follow.

Six Instructional Goals for Teaching Culture-Based Communicative Competence

Goal 1—Interest: The student shows curiosity about another culture (or another segment or subculture of one's own culture) and empathy toward its members.

Goal 2—Who: The student recognizes that role expectations and other social variables such as age, sex, social class, religion, ethnicity, and place of residence affect the way people speak and behave.

Goal 3—What: The student realizes that effective communication requires discovering the culturally conditioned images that are evoked in the minds of people when they think, act, and react to the world around them.

Goal 4—Where and When: The student recognizes that situational variables and convention shape behavior in important ways.

Goal 5—Why: The student understands that people generally act the way they do because they are using options their society allows for satisfying basic physical and psychological needs, and that cultural patterns are interrelated and tend mutually to support need satisfaction.

Goal 6—Exploration: The student can evaluate a generalization about a given culture in terms of the amount of evidence substantiating it, and has the skills needed to locate and organize information about a culture from the library, the mass media, people, and personal observation.

In other words, we can help the student develop interest in who in the culture in question did what, where and when, and why. (That summarizes the first five goals.) Further, we can help the student develop some sophistication in finding out more about the culture. (And this summarizes the sixth goal.)

These six goals involve skills that are associated with effective intercultural communication and that can be developed in our classes and workshops. Helping students achieve some degree of skill in each of these goals of cultural instruction can become an integral part of any program aimed at enhancing intercultural communication. These goals are explained and illustrated at length elsewhere (Seelye, 1994).

Implementing the Goals in the Language Classroom

How can teachers work their favorite unit on food into the framework of these six goals? Indeed, how do any of the activities generally carried out in the name of culture fit into the goals described above? The answer lies in the way teachers relate their favorite topics to a cultural goal.

One technique, by way of illustration, consists of asking pertinent questions about an artifact or photograph or magazine advertisement. You can relate practically anything to whichever of the six goals you wish, just by varying the questions you pose for students. For example, let's say you have an advertisement clipped from a magazine published in the target culture. To relate the clipping to Goal 1 (interest), you would ask what in the photo stimulates student curiosity, or ask about the student's willingness to become personally involved in some way with some activity or encounter in the photo. To relate the same clipping to Goal 2 (who), ask "Who does it or uses it?" Probe the relevance of social variables such as age, sex, social class, religion, or ethnicity to what is pictured in the photo.

Relating the clipping to Goal 3 (what), probe for any special connotations or reactions the designated people might have toward some aspect of the photo. Insight into this can be obtained by collecting associated visual images from other magazines or by interviewing people socialized in that culture. (Beware of The Fallacy of Projected Cognitive Similarity.)

Goal 4 (where and when) becomes relevant when you query the circumstances of doing or using what they see in the photo clipping. Is "it" associated with crises or mundane situations? With common or infrequent happenings? Is it associated with any particular events? Do people expect a conventional response to the situation? If so, what is the anticipated response?

To relate the clipping to Goal 5 (why), ask how the observed behavior may fit into the need-gratification system of the designated culture. What needs are being satisfied? What other options are available in that culture to gratify the same need?

Finally, to increase student skill in learning new things about the culture, Goal 6 (exploration), ask how the student can find out more about the aspect of the culture portrayed in the photo. What cultural generalizations can be hypothesized from the photo? How much evidence supports the generalization?

In the absence of instructional goals that focus on the cultural context of communication, what are the chances of developing the range of skills a student needs to understand and be understood in another culture?

References

Seelye, H. N. (1994). *Teaching culture: Strategies for intercultural communication*. (3rd rev. ed.). Lincolnwood, IL: National Textbook Co.

From Culture "Teaching" to Culture "Learning": Structures and Strategies for Increased Effectiveness

Carolyn Ryffel

The many contributors to this book reflect the increasing interest in culture learning activities for language education programs. Incorporating such activities, however, means much more than just adding them to a lesson plan. As Damon (1987) states in *Culture Learning:*

> Because [culture learning] is so deeply concerned with norms, values, beliefs, world views, and other aspects of subjective culture, it is a type of learning subject to the action of many variables and often accompanied by feelings of discomfort and even shock. (p. 216)

"Variables" and "discomfort" are key words here. Although we cannot totally eliminate the variables or discomfort, we can use culture learning activities more effectively by paying attention to two important areas: structure and strategies. First, by carefully *structuring* activities, we can ensure that they are more than just fun (or meaningless) games, that the emotional reactions (both ours and the students') are identified and addressed, and that meaningful learning occurs. Second, by using culturally sensitive *strategies* when adapting activities, moreover, we can decrease learner discomfort, reduce anxiety, and provide a safe environment by more closely conforming to what new students expect as appropriate classroom behavior. The discussion that follows addresses these interrelated issues of *structure* and *strategies*, applying the experiential learning cycle as a framework (structure) while offering suggestions for adapting and using activities (strategies).

On Structure and the Experiential Learning Cycle

Kolb's Experiential Learning Cycle (1984) is used as a basis for many teaching and training designs in the United States. Kolb's premise is that learning is incomplete unless an experience is processed by cycling through stages of reflection, generalization, and application. This framework is summarized below:

Experience: for data gathering

Processing: for completing the learning

Reflection: to establish what happened

Generalization: to identify learning

Application: to plan for the future

Activities commonly associated with experiential learning include self-assessment inventories, questionnaires, critical incidents, case studies, role plays, simulations, and excursions because most of these provide students with direct involvement and experience. Two caveats are in order, however, regarding experiential learning and its related techniques. The first caveat is that commercial materials based on the learning cycle often fail to complete all the stages. Most materials for teaching culture in the language classroom come from three sources: language texts, resources such as this book (which are few) providing carefully chosen activities, and books of activities from the intercultural field. Although the last source is especially rich, these materials must be used with special caution. The reasons for this are that they are primarily written for native English speakers in mind (specifically with U.S. Americans), and they presuppose a high level of expertise on the part of the facilitator, often omitting processing details.

The second caveat is that experiential teaching is primarily based on U.S. values—for example, learner centeredness, teacher as facilitator, learning by doing, verbalization, peer interaction, self-disclosure, and small-group work. Although similar notions are popping up elsewhere, many of these are part of the North American educational experience. In addition, many of these activities assume trust and risk taking among the participants because many experiential exercises by their very nature make students vulnerable. It is important to remember that a large portion of the world (and therefore many ESOL students) comes from collectivist cultures where relationships and harmony are of prime importance, maintained through indirect or less direct communication. Students from such cultures may have initial difficulty articulating opinions that could threaten group harmony, such as discussing sensitive, personal issues with others with whom they do not yet have a relationship. Strategies that guarantee students a rather safe environment for exploring potentially sensitive topics are therefore desirable.

Strategies for Using Culturally Sensitive Activities

The two main concerns regarding culturally sensitive activities are choosing and then adapting and using them, as appropriate to a given context. Let us first consider choice: Choice of an activity should depend on the following considerations:

1. logistics: that is, time constraints, space limitations, and materials required
2. aims and nature: for example, the objectives, the topic, the risk level, and the balance with other types of activities planned
3. the students: their language level, stage of cultural adjustment, preferred learning style(s), expectations for the classroom, and level of trust among the group and with the teacher
4. the teacher: the relationship with students, comfort level with culture learning activities, and expertise and experience

Once the activity is chosen, we need to consider how to adapt and use it properly. To ensure a risk-free environment that allows students to engage in the task, the following criteria should be considered:

1. instructions: Be clear and consistent when giving instructions; use clear language, providing examples or models. Give instructions both orally and in writing and, when in doubt, have the students restate their understanding of directions.
2. pacing: Allay anxiety by having set routines; proceed slowly in a step-by-step manner. Allow extra time to introduce new procedures.
3. teacher participation or intervention: Balance your desire for students to be the source of their own learning with their need for direction and help. Take care, however, not to interpret their silence necessarily as a lack of understanding; they may need more time to formulate

responses to the task; many cultures, in fact, value this type of reflection.

4. grouping: Be aware that even students from collectivist cultures are not necessarily comfortable in small groups because class groupings may be organized either arbitrarily or using different (and seemingly meaningless) criteria. In some cultures, it is not appropriate for people from different hierarchical levels to work together; if in doubt, let students organize themselves.

5. student participation: Again, this involves the issue of risk and trust. Some activities, such as role plays and simulations, are naturally high risk due to the uncertainty involved and the possibility of failure or exposure. Risk can be reduced by having the small group rather than an individual be responsible for a role or task. A volunteer group reporter, for example, can help take the burden off others unprepared for this task.

6. learning preferences: Vary tasks so that all learning style preferences are acknowledged; for example, alternate group work with individual work, or give students the option to work alone. Mix oral, reading, and writing tasks, and try occasionally to get away from the verbal altogether through art or sports.

7. discussion: To promote discussion use open-ended questions. Avoid yes/no questions except in groups with very low levels of English proficiency. Be sure that students have the vocabulary needed for the task.

8. students as source of information: To help students realize that they too are valid sources of information, write major ideas from discussions on newsprint. These ideas can then be transcribed, copied, and distributed to the class. Matching this with a professional article that makes similar points helps students gradually realize that they are also valid sources of information.

9. teacher as source of information: To help establish credibility and acceptance, teachers might meet students' more traditional expectations of teachers (at least initially), for example, by offering short lectures, guidance, and input; and then adjust teacher-student roles gradually over time, introducing more participatory type activities.

Conducting Effective Culture Learning Activities

Steps for planning and conducting effective culture learning activities include a focus on: (a) the aim(s), (b) the experience, and (c) the stages for processing the experience, in accordance with the experiential learning cycle. Let us consider each.

Aims

Having well-defined aims or objectives cannot be emphasized too much. Clear and well-defined aims help structure the activity for a particular time, with a particular group, and in a particular situation. Clear aims avoid unfocused classroom discussions that leave both the students and the teacher wondering at the end what was learned. It is especially easy in a language class to let students get caught up in a lively discussion whether or not it relates to the purposes. By keeping discussions on track, we maintain better control over the variables and the students' discomfort, and ultimately over the teaching-learning process itself.

Experience

Experience can be created through a teacher-generated activity or from the students' real-life experiences. The experience generates the data, the basis of the culture learning. This part of an activity need not be very long and, in fact, too much data makes it difficult to stay focused on the aim of the activity. Experiences may be varied and need not only be interactive group type activities. Reading an article, writing a story, listening to a lecture, or watching a video segment all provide valid experiences as long as students have a chance to interact with or react to the material at some point.

Processing

Processing the experience is as important as the experience itself and completes the learning cycle. As previously mentioned, this involves three stages: reflection, generalization, and application. None of these stages should be omitted and, taken together, they often take at least as much if not more time than the experience on which they are based. During the reflection stage, students are guided to think about what happened to them as individuals or within the dynamic of the group. Helpful questions are: What happened? What did you observe? What emotions, feelings, reactions did you experience? How were observations, reactions the same? Different? Responses typically include descriptions and reaction. Although students may want to go immediately to hypothesis and application, it is important to keep everyone focused for the moment on the experience itself.

The generalization stage now moves students from reflecting on what was learned to forming hypotheses and making associations. Helpful questions at this point are: What did you learn about yourself/the group/the situation? What do you understand better about yourself/the group? What does the experience mean for you? What does the experience relate to? How could the experience have been different?

Students are now ready for the application stage, which completes the learning cycle by projecting how new knowledge, awareness, or behavior is to be used. This stage is also the beginning of, and preparation for, the next experience. Questions here link the learning identified in the generalization stage with the future. For example:

- How can the learning be applied?

- What can be done differently?

- What will happen if nothing is done?

- What can be done the next time in a similar situation?

- What forces will help or hinder application?

Establishing a Safe and Supportive Environment

Most resources with "instructions to the teacher" suggest creating a nonjudgmental atmosphere in the classroom. This is a tough assignment, but it can be eased by considering the following: First, we must ourselves model behaviors and attitudes that are nonjudgmental. For this we need to be aware of our own cultural baggage—its values, beliefs, world view—and understand the extent to which we are a product of our own culture. Second, we should be clear about classroom norms and procedures and post them where they can be seen and referred to when necessary. Norms will probably be more closely followed when they are formulated with the help of students, but they should include respect for all opinions; a recognition that differences are not right or wrong, good or bad, but just different; the need for confidentiality (all discussions stay within the group); and full participation, which means being mentally engaged but not necessarily talking. Finally, no one—student or teacher—should be burdened with the role of being a spokesperson for a culture. Although everyone is a member of a culture, no one ever represents an entire cultural group.

Summary

Whether using the activities in this volume, those from a class text, or those from intercultural sources, the educational goal is to translate culture teaching into a culture learning experience for our students. If we consciously and conscientiously plan activities that proceed from experience through the various processing stages, there is a greater chance that culture learning will indeed occur. A careful choice of activities accompanied by careful structuring has the potential to decrease the uncontrolled variables and diminish discomfort for our students—and for us as well.

References and Further Reading

Damon, L. (1987). *Cultural learning: The fifth dimension in the language classroom.* Reading, MA: Addison-Wesley.

Fantini, A. E. (1993). Focus on process: An examination of the learning and teaching of intercultural communicative competence. In T. Gochenour (Ed.), *Beyond experience: The experiential approach to cross-cultural education* (2nd ed., pp. 45–53). Yarmouth, ME: Intercultural Press.

Gaston, J. (1984). *Cultural awareness teaching techniques.* Brattleboro, VT: Pro Lingua.

Gaw, B. (1979). Processing questions: An aid to completing the learning cycle. In J. E. Jones & J. W. Pfeiffer (Eds.), *The 1979 annual handbook for group facilitators* (pp. 147–153). La Jolla, CA: University Associates.

Kolb, D. A. (1984). *Experiential learning: Experience as the source of learning and development.* Englewood Cliffs, NJ: Prentice-Hall.

Janeway, A. (1977). The experiential approach to cross-cultural education. In D. Batchelder & E. G. Warner (Eds.), *Beyond experience: The experiential approach to cross-cultural education* (pp. 5–8). Brattleboro, VT: The Experiment Press.

Paige, R., & Martin J. (1983). Ethical issues and ethics in intercultural training. In D. Landis & R. Brislin (Eds.), *Handbook of intercultural training* (vol. 1, pp. 36–30). Elmsford, NY: Pergamon Press.

Pepin, C. (1993). A short guide to designing and conducting an experiential exercise. In T. Gochenour (Ed.), *Beyond experience: The experiential approach to cross-cultural education* (2nd ed., pp. 73–77). Yarmouth, ME: Intercultural Press.

Ramsey, S. (in press). Adapting intercultural methods for training across cultures. In S. Fowler & M. Mumford (Eds.), *Intercultural sourcebook* (vol. 2). Yarmouth, ME: Intercultural Press.

Checking Teacher Culture/ Intercultural Competencies: The YOGA Form*

Alvino E. Fantini

The acronym *YOGA* stands for "Your Objectives, Guidelines and Assessment." I created this form as a monitoring aid for teacher development. As the name implies, it is intended to help in three ways:

- by clarifying objectives for the intern (in a preservice case) or for the practicing teacher (in an in-service case)
- by providing guidelines for periodic monitoring over time (e.g., during the intern's practicum or for a longer duration in the case of the practicing teacher)
- by establishing a common assessment procedure for use at various moments by both intern/teacher and observer/mentor/supervisor.

In other words, the form addresses formative, summative, and normative concerns, focusing on: how the individual is getting along, where the individual is at the moment, and how the individual compares with competencies commonly recognized by the profession.

For convenience and clarity, teacher competencies are grouped into six commonly recognized professional areas:

- Interpersonal Relations
- Culture/Intercultural Teacher Competencies
- Language/Linguistics
- Language Acquisition and Learning
- Language Teaching (which includes curriculum design and lesson planning, implementation, and assessment)
- Professionalism

---

*Adapted from "Teacher Assessment," by Alvino E. Fantini, 1993. In D. Freeman, with S. Cornwell (Eds.), *New ways in teacher education* (pp. 43–55). Alexandria, VA: TESOL. Excerpt reprinted with permission.

A full explanation and the complete form covering all six areas can be found in another volume of the New Ways in TESOL series (see Fantini, 1993). For our present purpose, however, we are concerned primarily with the second area: Culture/Intercultural Teacher Competencies. The checklist (see excerpt from the form below) can help teachers rethink how they are fulfilling competencies in this area.

The form may be used by interns as well as practicing teachers. For the intern, the form is provided before or early in the internship period and is reviewed periodically throughout the experience and again at the end of the experience. Given its emphasis on self-monitoring, the individual being observed uses the form first to conduct a self-assessment. This is followed by observation and evaluation conducted by the visitor. These separate evaluations are compared and contrasted to help focus dialogue on varying perspectives of the teaching experience. The practitioner and observer/ evaluator conclude with a summary of strengths and areas for improve- ment, prioritizing objectives for the next time period. A similar process unfolds where a practicing teacher is involved, with the additional recogni- tion that evaluations may also have administrative consequences (e.g., contract renewal, advancement, pay raises, suggestions for further training). Because the form is used at various times, different marking systems should be employed on each occasion to track development; for example, a checkmark ($\checkmark$) may be used the first time, a circle ($\bigcirc$) the next, and a triangle ($\triangle$) the third (or different colored markings might be used). Self- assessment aside, a second perspective and the dialogue exchange are both quite important to teacher development. Each completes the form sepa- rately, followed by an exchange in which impressions, insights, and suggestions are discussed.

No matter when or how used, the form is designed to nurture reflection, to aid analysis and synthesis—important stages in clinical supervision, and to orient future action. The exchange between teacher and observer/ assessor is an important dimension of this cycle of reflection, analysis, synthesis, and action. Emphasis is on the conferencing and the perceptions each contributes, rather than on who is right or wrong. Analysis and synthesis result in a profile of the teacher's strengths and identification of areas for future development. An action plan for future work might include reading, action research, focused practice, developing new techniques, revising a course plan, or taking additional course work in specified areas.

Because the rating system is designed to chart development over time, there should be evidence of: (a) minimally acceptable performance; (b) movement or progress; and (c) improvement in specific directions/areas, agreed upon by the person observed and the observer/evaluator. The key used is as follows (with +/- to indicate intermediate points):

0 = NA (Not applicable), NO (Not observed), or See written comment(s)
1 = Room for growth/development
2 = Acceptable
3 = Competent

Following is an excerpt from Part II of the YOGA Form, which lists specific teacher competencies in culture and intercultural dimensions of his or her work:

II. Culture/Intercultural Teacher Competencies

Inclusion of sociocultural dimension in the lessons:
- is aware of and attentive to
  sociolinguistic variables   0 / - 1 + / - 2 + / - 3 +
- uses appropriate target language
  social interactional activities   0 / - 1 + / - 2 + / - 3 +
- addresses target language culture in
  different content and context
  areas: readings, discussions, topics, etc.   0 / - 1 + / - 2 + / - 3 +

Presence of cultural dimension in classroom dynamics:
- is sensitive to/respects student
  cultural differences   0 / - 1 + / - 2 + / - 3 +
- uses the cultural diversity of
  students to advantage   0 / - 1 + / - 2 + / - 3 +
- fosters students' interest in and understanding
  of the target culture   0 / - 1 + / - 2 + / - 3 +

- creates opportunities for students to experience the target culture (not just the "methodological" culture)   0 / - 1 + / - 2 + / - 3 +
- fosters students' respect for cultural diversity   0 / - 1 + / - 2 + / - 3 +

Inclusion of intercultural dimension
- compares and contrasts target and native culture(s)   0 / - 1 + / - 2 + / - 3 +
- explores intercultural processes (stages, options, consequences)   0 / - 1 + / - 2 + / - 3 +
- responds to intercultural conflicts if they arise   0 / - 1 + / - 2 + / - 3 +
- explores impact of language on intercultural entry   0 / - 1 + / - 2 + / - 3 +

Aware of/sensitive and responsive to intercultural challenges of the teaching situation:
- in the classroom   0 / - 1 + / - 2 + / - 3 +
- in the institution   0 / - 1 + / - 2 + / - 3 +
- in the community   0 / - 1 + / - 2 + / - 3 +
- and in the target culture (if applicable)   0 / - 1 + / - 2 + / - 3 +

Others: _____   0 / - 1 + / - 2 + / - 3 +
_____   0 / - 1 + / - 2 + / - 3 +
_____   0 / - 1 + / - 2 + / - 3 +

References

Fantini, A. E. (1993). Teacher assessment. In D. Freeman, with S. Cornwell (Eds.), *New ways in teacher education* (pp. 43–55). Alexandria, VA: TESOL.

Developing Intercultural Competence: A Process Approach Framework[*]

Alvino E. Fantini

Given the expanded focus of language education to include preparing individuals to function effectively and appropriately in a new culture, developing intercultural communicative competence emerges as an important goal. Language proficiency must be developed within the context of "appropriate" behaviors, determined by the norms of a specific culture. To achieve this, both the target language and culture must be explored.

To maintain the focus on culture/intercultural dimensions as well as language, a process approach (PA) framework may be a helpful device. Seven stages are outlined that, when taken together, suggest a process for developing course syllabi and individual lesson plans:

1. presentation of new material
2. practice of new material within a limited and controlled context
3. explanation or elucidation of the grammar rules behind the material, where necessary or useful (more appropriate for adolescent and older learners than for young children)
4. transposition and use of new material (in accumulation with other materials previously learned by the students) into freer, less controlled contexts and more spontaneous conversation
5. sociolinguistic exploration of the interrelationships of social context and language use, emphasizing the appropriateness of specific language styles (as opposed to grammaticality) (see Part III of this volume for sociolinguistic techniques)

---

*Adapted from "Focus on Process: An Examination of the Learning and Teaching of Communicative Competence," by A. E. Fantini and W. P. Dant, 1993. In T. Gochenour (Ed.), *Beyond experience* (2nd ed., pp. 79–96). Yarmouth, ME: Intercultural Press. Used with permission of Intercultural Press.

6. culture exploration for determining appropriate interactional strategies and behaviors, while also learning about values, beliefs, customs, and so on of the target culture (see Part IV for culture techniques)
7. intercultural exploration for comparing and contrasting the target culture with the student's native culture (see Part V for intercultural techniques)

Most teachers are already familiar with Stages 1–4 (usually preceded by a warm-up phase); less obvious perhaps are Stages 5–7. Their inclusion, however, ensures that language work is always complemented by explicit attention to sociolinguistic aspects, cultural aspects, and the comparing and contrasting of target and native linguacultures. Because language texts generally focus on language structure and, more commonly in recent years, on communication (Stages 1–4), the teacher is often left to develop Stage 5–7 activities alone.

The PA framework lays out a complete process leading to intercultural communication (ICC), clarifying the objectives of each learning stage and appropriate activities along the way. The framework, then, helps in selecting, sequencing, and evaluating learning/teaching activities. Activities can be chosen because of their match with the learning objectives of each stage, rather than drawn at random from a bag of tricks. The framework guides the teacher in choosing from and using the many activities presented in this volume that deal with Stages 5–7 (in addition to activities for general exploration of the nexus between language and culture in Part II), on the assumption that teachers already have a repertoire of Stage 1–4 activities.

A few additional thoughts about using the PA framework as a guide may be helpful. It should be emphasized that one need not necessarily follow the sequence of the stages as they appear in the framework itself. In other words, although one could begin with Stage 1 and continue linearly through Stage 7, one could also start at any other point. And, in fact, the process is cyclical; that is, the stages should be built cyclically throughout the syllabus and lesson plans. Neither should one get the impression that all seven stages must be covered in a single lesson; rather, several lesson units may be required before starting the cycle anew. My own preference, in fact, is to start with Stage 6 (or possibly 5 or even 7), providing a target cultural event as a starting point for the language lesson that follows and flows from it. In this way, the language lesson is framed within a cultural context. Teachers will also readily discover that some activities overlap several stages all at once, whereas others neatly focus on a specific stage. Finally, the teacher with deductive preferences may choose to present Stage 3 before Stages 2 and 4 (in other words, grammar work before practice and use). The inductive teacher, on the other hand, may prefer presenting Stage 2 before Stage 3 (i.e., presentation and practice followed by explicit rules). Rather than sequence and cycle, what remains important throughout is that the teacher address language and culture.

Summary

A PA framework serves to select teaching activities, materials, and techniques, and to ensure that all aspects of intercultural competence are addressed. It encourages synthesis of all that is known about learning and teaching. Its implementation is based on optimum matching of the student, the teacher, the context, and the activity.

The framework below illustrates some activities appropriate to each of the seven stages, just as the activities that follow later in this volume provide useful ideas for responding to Stages 5–7.

A Process Approach Framework:
A Syllabus and/or Lesson Schema

I. Presentation of New Material

    1. A full or abbreviated dialogue
    2. A two-line exchange (question/answer)
    3. Manipulation of cuisenaire rods (à la Silent Way)
    4. _____
    5. _____
    6. _____

II. Practice in Context

    1. Pattern practice (all types of drills)
    2. Controlled narrative and questions
    3. Structured conversation or other activity
    4. _____
    5. _____
    6. _____

III. Grammar Exploration

    1. Grammatical explanation of rules
    2. Students figure out rules (à la Counseling Language Learning)
    3. Use of grammar reference books
    4. _____
    5. _____
    6. _____

IV. Transposition (or Use)

    1. Unstructured or free conversation
    2. Manipulation of visual aids, objects, and so on
    3. Free narratives
    4. Games
    5. _____
    6. _____

V. Sociolinguistic Exploration

    1. Research aspects of language use
    2. Simulations and role play (with varying social factors such as age, sex, role)
    3. Practice interactional strategies (e.g., greeting, commands, interrupting)
    4. _____
    5. _____
    6. (see Part III of this volume for more sociolinguistic techniques)

VI. Target Culture Exploration

 1. Cultural operations (e.g., making a peanut butter and jelly sandwich)
 2. Panel and/or group discussion of cultural themes (e.g., family unit, time concepts, respect systems, humor, personal hygiene)
 3. Viewing video segments of events in the target culture
 4. _____
 5. _____
 6. (see Part IV of this volume for more culture exploration techniques)

VII. Intercultural Exploration

 1. Comparing and contrasting target culture and students' own culture(s)
 2. Exploring cultural contact and entry
 3. Exploring causes for culture shock/stress
 4. _____
 5. _____
 6. (see Part V of this volume for more intercultural exploration techniques)

References and Further Reading

Fantini, A. E., & Dant, W. P. (1993). Focus on process: An examination of the learning and teaching of communicative competence. In T. Gochenour (Ed.), *Beyond experience* (2nd ed., pp. 79-96). Yarmouth, ME: Intercultural Press.

Part II: Activities for Language-Culture Exploration

Aba-Zak: A World View Exercise*

Levels
Intermediate +

Aims
Become aware of the connections between language, culture, and world view

Class Time
$1^1/_2$–2 hours

Preparation Time
30 minutes

Resources
1 envelope of Aba-Zak objects/group

Most people take language for granted, unaware that their native tongue is not merely a "neutral" communication system, but rather a pervasive medium that influences every aspect of their lives. This unawareness is probably due to the fact that we develop our language ability so early in life and seldom need to reflect on it. Not only does grappling with communication through another language offer an opportunity to learn about another way of life, but even more importantly, it raises questions about one's own language, culture, and world view.

Aba-Zak is an experiential exercise designed to explore the notion of world view; that is, the idea that different societies perceive and interpret the world in various ways. This is manifest in their culture and encoded in the language they speak. Languages, then, provide a sort of road map for discovering the way speakers understand and interpret reality. Because of the abstract nature of language, however, getting at the concept of world view is often difficult. This exercise helps create such an opportunity.

In the first phase, participants explore the relationship of language and culture to world view. In the second phase, one member of each group "visits" another group, thereby simulating a cross-cultural contact and entry experience. Finally, after returning to the "native" culture, students reflect on the strategies they used and the results obtained in terms of their intercultural communicative competence, as well as compare and contrast *etic* (outsider) and *emic* (insider) views of the two cultures.

*From A. E. Fantini (Ed.), 1995, Spring. Special Focus Issue on Language, Culture and World View, *International Journal of Intercultural Relations, 19*, 297–302. Adapted with permission from Elsevier Science Ltd.

Procedure

Phase 1

1. Prepare enough sets of Aba-Zak objects for your class. Instructions appear in the Appendix.
2. Divide the class into groups ("cultures") of three to six students each, depending on the size of the class. A minimum of two groups is needed, although any number of groups can be involved.
3. Ask students to organize their group in terms of how they wish to accomplish the task, for example, who will do what, how will decisions be made, and so on.
4. Give to each group an envelope containing the objects of their "world." After examining the contents, each group determines which characteristics of the objects are of importance/interest and then proceeds to categorize the items accordingly (e.g., in terms of color, size, shape or other traits).
5. Groups should invent a name/label for each category of items. They may also organize them further on the basis of a secondary characteristic, labeling each subcategory as they proceed. (In naming categories and subcategories, the group may wish to show relationships between them. For example, *zak* could serve as the name for a category of squares; *aba* and *baba* added to the root *zak* (*aba-zak, baba-zak*) could represent their colors: red and blue.)
6. Finally, each group should determine if all its members will use the same words for categories, or whether different members of the "society" should use different expressions. For example, will both sexes use the same words? Persons of higher/lower status? What about individuals with blond/brown hair?

Phase 2

1. When the initial phase is completed, have one member of each group leave to visit another group (or "culture"). Visitors should explore the new society and try to learn as much as possible about the host culture. However, visitors must use only the language of their own team, and hosts must use only their tongue. (If time is limited, you may permit them to use English after attempting to communicate with no common tongue for a few minutes.)

2. Visitors should try to find out whether word equivalents exist in the host culture for words in their own language. If words in the host language do not easily translate, try to find out why and what words in the host language "mean."

Phase 3

1. After about 15 minutes, visitors should return to their original group.
2. Have students recount in their original groups what they learned about their hosts' culture and language (from their own perspective).

Phase 4

1. After completing the first three phases of this exercise, debrief the exercise by discussing the following questions with the entire class.
    ● How successful were you in being accepted by your hosts? How important was language to that process?
    ● What helped/hindered cultural acceptance?
    ● Was it difficult to find word equivalents? Why?
    ● How did the hosts' culture (and organization of their world) influence what they perceived and attended to? Also, how did language reflect perception and organization of their world view, reinforce it, and give it shape?
    ● Contrast what objects were regarded as important/unimportant to your own culture and the host culture (what features were recognized, what ignored; e.g., was the missing corner on the one triangle significant?). Comment on the different categories and values given to the various objects.
    ● How did the way groups were organized (societally) affect how different members of the same culture referred to the same thing? Conversely, how did differentiated speech reflect and reinforce any subgroups?
    ● How did your understanding of the host culture match that society's own description of itself? (At this point you may need to have members from two different groups compare and contrast some aspect.)

- What can you say about language-culture determinism and relativity (i.e., how one's native language-culture influences and affects one's world view and how different languages-cultures create different visions of the world)?
- Finally, discuss world view, that is, how are speakers, their language, and what they mean, interrelated? Relate this to other intercultural experiences you may have had.

Caveats and Options

1. This exercise can be conducted with any size class, provided that students are divided into smaller groups of no more than four to six people. Take care to set up the small groups and to provide all instructions before handing out envelopes. Once you have explained the task, do not answer further questions while the exercise is in progress.
2. Carefully monitor the time allotted to each phase of the exercise, allowing adequate though not excessive time for each part. Announce 5 minutes and again 1 minute before the end of each phase as it is concluding so that groups can pace their work.
3. Upon completion of the exercise, keep small groups intact while debriefing them about the entire exercise. Use the debriefing questions to help participants focus on each aspect of the exercise and thereby come to a more explicit understanding of the intricacies of world view.
4. Depending on the level of the group, you may simplify or further complicate this activity by including more, or fewer, objects and variables. You may also highlight or omit various phases of the activity in accordance with your own aims.

References and Further Reading

Fantini, A. E. et al. (1984). *Cross-cultural orientation: A guide for leaders and educators.* Brattleboro, VT: The Bookstore, School for International Training.

Fantini, A. E. (Ed.). (1995, Spring). Special focus issue on language, culture and world view, *International Journal of Intercultural Relations, 19*.

Appendix: Instructions for Making Aba-Zak Sets

Use the directions and template below to make sets of Aba-Zak objects for each group involved in the exercise.

1. Photocopy the template on page 52. You may wish to enlarge the size of the template when copying.
2. Using the photocopy, cut out the 13 figures and use as patterns to make three of each object except the circle. Discard the dark areas. Make each set of the same three objects in a different color (e.g., one each red, green, and blue box; one each red, green, and blue triangle). Then cut out one circle on white paper.
3. Next cut a small and not too noticeable tip off of one large triangle and mark the symbol # on one of the small triangles.
4. Compile the 13 items and join with a paper clip. Place this packet of objects on a plain sheet of paper. Add some tea grains randomly. Fold the sheet in three like a letter and place it in an envelope.
5. Be sure to make one complete set (i.e., envelope plus contents) for each group involved. Make sure sets for each group are identical.

Continued

Template for Making Aba-Zak Sets

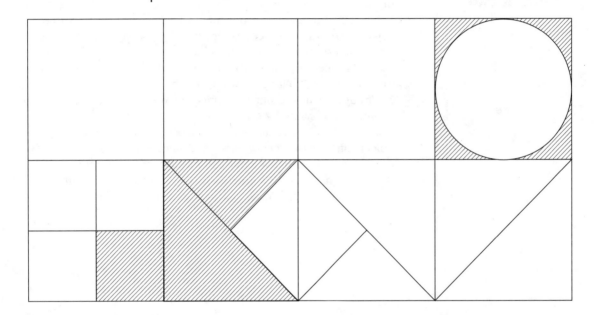

Contributor

Alvino E. Fantini, senior faculty member at the School for International Training, Brattleboro, Vermont, in the United States, is a past president of SIETAR International (Society for Intercultural Education, Training, and Research) and an international consultant on matters of language and intercultural communications.

Culture Exploration: A NAPI-KEPRA Framework*

Levels
Any

Aims
Maximize learning of
the target culture
Investigate components
of culture while
appreciating their
interconnectedness
Develop a culture
exploration framework
for future use
Consider the process
aspect of culture
investigation as relevant
to culture contact
Use language in real
contexts and in the
context of culture
learning

Class Time
Variable

Preparation Time
20 minutes

Resources
Handouts

Many activities offer a way of exploring specific aspects of culture, but this exercise is powerful in that it provides a way of tracking those aspects while also appreciating their interconnectedness. In other words, this suggests a scheme that ensures a more holistic view of the target culture at both the present moment (synchrony) and through time (diachrony)—from the historical past to the future. It also requires participants to engage in activities with native speakers outside of class and to take both passive roles (especially low-level students) and active roles (intermediate- to advanced-level students). The framework, sometimes referred to as *NAPI-KEPRA* (its acronym), affords us an ongoing way of visiting and revisiting the target culture, deepening our understanding and involvement at each turn. It draws on the students' current knowledge and involves them in doing further research by using local resources as available (in an EFL situation) or going out into the actual community (in an ESL situation) for further exploration.

Procedure

1. Identify resources to be used for the task (whether materials, if EFL, or the local community, if ESL), delineate the geographical area for the task (ESL), and discuss strategies for observing or interviewing people.
2. On a flip chart, or in handouts, give students a framework to aid in their investigation (see Appendix). Explain that the framework serves

---

*This exercise originally appeared in "Exploring the Community," by Alvino E. Fantini, 1984. In *Getting the whole picture: Part III* (pp. 22-53). Intercultural Exchange Series. Brattleboro, VT: The Bookstore, School for International Training. Adapted with permission from the author.

as a simplified map of culture, identifying the givens or elements of culture listed down the left-hand column, and the systems, processes, or organizations across the top. Give examples from one or two grids where these intersect. For example, in the investigation of a host culture family, People and Kinship intersect; religious accoutrements involve Religion and Artifacts, and a local Youth Club might involve Associations and People. Double-check the students' understanding by having them give additional examples.

3. Divide students into pairs, or teams of three or four, and have them decide what area(s) they wish to investigate, where, and how.

4. Brainstorm strategies they can use to find out what they want to know (from passive and observational approaches for students with limited proficiency), to active and participatory approaches (for those with higher proficiencies).

5. Have students compose typical questions they might ask.

6. Discuss with students how their approach, style, and language level may affect the task and the results they obtain.

7. After students do the field investigation and return to class, give them time to organize their reports for presentation to the entire class. As each group makes its report, check off on the framework which grid they are speaking about to illustrate which aspects of culture have or have not been addressed.

8. Other debriefing questions might include
   - content (What did they find out?)
   - process aspect (How did it go? How did they feel?)
   - framework check (What did they investigate? or not? Why?)
   - *etic* versus *emic* perspectives (What did they report about the target culture versus what natives might report about themselves?)
   - students' level of knowledge (How might they go on to probe the culture more deeply?)
   - contact with the host culture (What are the possible interests/reasons students might have for entering this culture? What is the degree of possible entry?)
   - students' self-identity vis à vis the target culture
   - students' motivations (integrative vs. instrumental) for entering the target culture

- students' approach and speech style (How does their level of proficiency influence contact?)
- problem areas and additional language needs for the next bout

Caveats and Options

1. If you prefer to conduct this activity inductively, then omit Step 2 (presentation of the NAPI-KEPRA framework) and have the students explore the community without providing a structure. In other words, the task is open-ended the first time around and the framework is constructed during their presentation of content. It can then help clarify what they investigated as well as what they left out and can be useful for the next time they go out to explore.
2. Students with no or low-level proficiency can explore the community and conduct observation-type activities; students with higher levels can take more active roles.
3. Adding historicity, that is, past or future dimensions to the framework (see Appendix), makes the task even more elaborate. Students can consider any one of the grids in terms of how it was in the past (e.g., past month, past year, 50 years ago) and of the future (e.g., next month, next year, 50 years from now).
4. At more advanced levels, you can lead a discussion on related topics such as culture, definitions of culture, culture components and interrelatedness, synchronic and diachronic dimensions of culture (as it is now in the present and as it was/will be through time), etic and emic perspectives, cross-cultural contact, entry options and consequences, individual motivations for learning the target linguaculture, cultural comparisons, and more.

References and Further Reading

Batchelder, D. (1993). The drop-off. In T. Gochenour (Ed.), *Beyond experience* (2nd ed., pp. 135–141). Yarmouth, ME: Intercultural Press.

Fantini, A. E. (Ed.). (1984). Exploring the community. In *Getting the whole picture: Part III* (pp. 22–53). Intercultural Exchange Series. Brattleboro, VT: The Bookstore, School for International Training.

Appendix: The NAPI-KEPRA Framework

	Kinship	Economics	Politics	Religion	Associations
Natural Environment					
Artifacts					
People					
Information/ Communication					
Historicity (i.e., +/- time dimension / past and/or future)					

Contributor

Alvino E. Fantini, senior faculty member at the School for International Training, Brattleboro, Vermont, in the United States, is a past president of SIETAR International (Society for Intercultural Training, Research, and Education) and an international consultant on matters of language and intercultural communications.

Artifacts, Sociofacts, Mentifacts: A Sociocultural Framework

Levels
Intermediate +

Aims
Identify the three
interrelated dimensions
of culture and specific
examples within each
Deepen understanding
about the nature of
language and culture
and their inter-
connectedness
Practice language
appropriate to the tasks

Class Time
30 minutes–1 hour

Preparation Time
30 minutes

Resources
Handouts

This activity makes use of a basic sociological framework to enhance the teaching of language and culture in the classroom. The framework presents three interrelated aspects of culture—artifacts (things people make), sociofacts (how people come together and for what purpose), and mentifacts (what people think or believe). The three dimensions are interrelated: No matter what dimension one begins with, the other two are always present and available for exploration to help deepen one's understanding of language/culture. For example, if one considers any object or item, such as a sandwich (or a cross, a vacuum cleaner, a catcher's mitt . . .), one can consider first of all what a sandwich is (e.g., lunch, snack, bread and coldcuts), what people (who), when, and how use a sandwich (e.g., working people, students, for picnics, bite size for cocktails), and finally what the notion of sandwich represents or means (e.g., portable, inexpensive, quick, common fare). The framework encourages language-culture exploration that goes beyond merely considering a cultural item, but more importantly the significance and social uses related to the item.

Procedure

1. First ask students to identify cultural items, either of the target culture or their own.
2. As they generate a list, write the words on the board, grouping them in three columns (in terms of artifacts, sociofacts, and mentifacts without using these labels just yet). For example: *taco, pencil, typewriter, wedding, proverbs, myths, tools, beliefs, great books, values, party* might be listed as follows:

taco	wedding	beliefs
pencil	party	values
typewriter		
proverbs		
myths		
tools		
great books		

(Students typically list more artifact items than sociofacts or mentifacts.)

3. Ask students to consider what the items in each column have in common. Then add the headings—Artifacts, Sociofacts, Mentifacts—and explain the meaning of each.

4. Have students pick any item from any column—or add new items—and discuss how any item in any one column has its counterparts in the other two. For example, if one chooses the item *wedding,* one can then discuss and list the various artifacts related to the social occasion of a wedding in one's own culture or the target culture and then discuss the significance or meaning of each.

5. After discussing the relationship between artifacts, sociofacts, and mentifacts, have students compare and contrast these in their own culture and the target culture, as well as the language expressions connected with them. Take special note of where relationships among the three dimensions and the language expressions used for each do not correspond across cultures.

Caveats and Options

1. The language used may be either the target language or the students' native tongue(s), depending on their proficiency level and the main objective(s) of the lesson.

2. You may follow this activity with an out-of-class assignment in which students choose either an artifact (e.g., sandwich), a sociofact (e.g., wedding), or a mentifact (e.g., some belief or value) and investigate with native speakers the various dimensions and the appropriate language expressions that accompany each.

3. Once this framework is well understood, you can use it throughout the course as a reference point as well as to deepen and expand any cultural topic that may come up.

4. Use the handouts in the Appendix to continue class discussion on culture (Handout 1), or to work further on language or culture (Handouts 2 and 3). Handout 2 can be used to work through a sample together, and Handout 3, which is blank, can be used by students to do their own analysis.

Appendix

Handout 1: More About Culture

1. Culture is created by people.
2. It exists in time and space, that is, in an environment in which human beings act and react upon their space, the time dimension, their thoughts about things, themselves and others.
3. It has several components:
   - artifacts (that which is made, created, produced)
   - sociofacts (the ways in which people organize their society and relate to one another)
   - mentifacts (the ideas, beliefs, and values that people hold)
   Together, these components of any culture account for any and all of the following:

manners	customs	beliefs
ceremonies	rituals	tools
laws (written	institutions	religious
and unwritten)	knowledge	beliefs
myths and legends	social taboos	values
concept of self	art and	language
ideas and thought patterns	art objects	models
ideals	customs	food
accepted ways of behaving	holidays	books

4. The whole of culture is greater that the sum of its individual parts, and the parts are interrelated. We can say that a tool (artifact) involves the custom (sociofact) for the use of that tool, and that the custom involves the ideas or concepts behind it (mentifact).
5. Culture is learned. It is not genetically transmitted as are racial characteristics. We learn to speak, think, and act the way we do because of the people and the culture that surround us.

Handout 2: A Language/Culture Practice Outline

1. Artifact: An object from the target culture

Students should be able to:
- give or ask for the name of an object (if unknown)
- give or ask for a brief description of the components, materials, size . . .
- give or ask for some historical background

Related Language Practice

Examples:
- involves the use of basic interrogatives (e.g., what, why, where)
- verbs (e.g., to be, to make)
- structures (e.g., present/past tenses, prepositions)
- other (e.g., pronouns, agreement, gender, number)

2. Sociofact

Students should be able to:
- explain or ask for instances when this object is used
- tell or explore who uses the object and for what purpose
- explore a social explanation of the object

Related Language Practice

Examples:
- more interrogatives (e.g., who, when)
- narrate and describe in the present tense
- use appropriate adjectives

3. Mentifact

Students should be able to:
- determine the significance of the object and its use
- explore the cultural importance for people of the target culture
- understand any values, beliefs, rituals, related to the object

Related Language Practice

Examples:
- ask/answer questions of why and why not
- make statements with conditional (if appropriate)
- review and practice all basic interrogatives

Handout 3: Sample Student Practice Sheet

1. Artifact (what)

   Related Language Practice

2. Sociofact (who/when/where/how)

   Related Language Practice

3. Mentifact (why/meaning)

   Related Language Practice

Contributors

Beatriz C. de Fantini is a faculty member of the Master of Arts in Teaching (MAT) program and also the director of the Language and Culture Center at the School for International Training, Brattleboro, Vermont, in the United States. Alvino E. Fantini is a senior faculty member of the MAT program and also the director of Bilingual-Multicultural Education at the same institution.

Fantasy Island: A Language and Cultural Awareness Exercise

Levels
Any

Aims
Become aware of
critical aspects of their
own and other cultures
by attempting to create
aspects of an imaginary
culture and develop an
understanding for
differences found across
cultures
Investigate commu-
nicative strategies
Learn something about
the nature of language

Class Time
2 + hours

Preparation Time
30 minutes

Resources
Assorted paper, colored
pens or paints, crepe
paper, fabric scraps,
yarn or string, staplers,
adhesive tape, and other
objects

Working in groups of 6–12 participants, aged 10 years to adult, groups devise certain characteristics of a "culture" for presentation to the other groups. The number and extent of the characteristics requested may depend on the time available as well as the ages and experience of group members.

Procedure

1. Divide participants into groups of 6–12 members each. Make sure that participants are seated comfortably for a short discussion.
2. Advise each group that they will be creating their own "island," with specific characteristics such as:
   - climate (a sketched map of the island to indicate differing climatic conditions in different areas)
   - housing
   - national/typical dress
   - typical foods/meals
   - national/folk dance or song
   - basic vocabulary (social greetings, words used to describe items listed above, sufficient to present their new "culture" to other groups)
3. Advise each group that they will be required to present their "Fantasy Island" to other participants at the end of the session.
4. Members of a group should work together for an hour to produce sketches of their imaginary homeland and to consider how the climate and resources may affect the type of housing and the typical food of their new culture. They can also devise a national dance and create some basic musical accompaniment. If suitable resources are available (e.g., paper, scrap fabrics, coloring pens or paints, scissors,

staplers), they can create a national costume to wear in the presentation of their culture. Considerable discussion may arise in the generation of a basic vocabulary, which should be different from the language of any of the group members.

5. Adequate time should be allowed at the end of the session for each group to present the characteristics of its new culture to others, or presentations can take place in a subsequent session.

Caveats and Options

1. Do some informal evaluation during the presentation to other groups and encourage any discussions that arise from this.
2. With appropriate guidance, participants can be helped to consider how the physical environment they suggested (e.g., climate, housing) affected other aspects of the invented culture and thus the relevance of local environment to real cultures.
3. Participants can be guided to think about how their own experience of aspects of the culture in which they normally live influenced their input and their expectations of the culture they were asked to create.
4. This activity is often used in multinational residential camps for 11-year-old children, where each of four groups might have one representative from each of about 10 different countries, working with two or three adults. As the children do not always share a common language, a wide variety of communication strategies are normally invented by the participants. The activity is useful in generating awareness of aspects of culture that are shared by participants from different nations, in learning strategies for communicating and developing insights into how languages work, and in helping them respect the ways in which the cultures of other participants differ from their own.
5. Mature adolescents and adults may move on to consider:
   - what we actually mean by *culture*
   - what would be the defining characteristics of a culture
   - what was learned about communication
   - what was learned about language
   - how and why we should show respect for aspects of other cultures
   - implications of the breakdown of cultural respect

6. In a group of ESOL students, the initial communication may be easier, depending on their level of proficiency. However, it may be necessary to make the evaluation more explicit in order to demonstrate aspects of intercultural awareness and respect.

Contributor

Jennifer Watson is chair of the International Educational Development and Research Committee for Children's International Summer Villages (CISV International), a volunteer organization promoting cross-cultural friendships and international understanding with international headquarters in Newcastle, England.

Piglish: A Language Learning Exercise*

Levels
Intermediate +

Aims
Experience the process
of learning a new
language
Identify various
strategies for learning
language
Develop empathy for
persons speaking in a
second language
Explore aspects of the
relationship between
limited second/foreign
language proficiency,
culture, and world view

Class Time
40–90 minutes

Preparation Time
30 minutes

Resources
Handouts

This exercise allows participants to explore the process of second language-culture acquisition. The exercise was first conceived of by Dan Edwards of Training Resources Group, Washington, DC, who wrote the first draft of the Piglish story as a fairy tale context for a language simulation. The vocabulary, grammar, and training methodology were tested with volunteers and revised by program staff at Youth for Understanding International Exchange before this present version was issued.

Procedure

Part 1: Introduction

1. Tell the group that this is a lighthearted exercise designed to let everyone experience what it is like to learn a new language.
2. Ask the group about their language learning experiences. What was the experience like? Was it fun? What was hard? Easy? Why?
3. Tell participants that they are going to have the opportunity to learn a new language, one they probably have not encountered before. After practicing and speaking this language, they will have an opportunity to talk about the process of learning Piglish.

Part 2: The Piglish Story

1. Introduce the Piglish language by giving some of the background of its origin. Use the information in the first paragraph of the introduction in Handout 2 (see Appendix).

---

*This exercise originally appeared in *Learning About Language,* by Volunteers in Intercultural Programs, Youth for Understanding International Exchange, 1989. Intercultural Communication Series. Washington, DC: Author. Reprinted with permission. Copyright © Youth for Understanding, Washington, DC.

2. Explain that a favorite story of the "Piglers" (early society groups who spoke Piglish) is "The Three Little Pigs." Use Handout 1 (see Appendix) to provide the story line. You need to have a single simple story that everyone can follow in the exercise. An alternative would be to ask one of the participants to tell the story for the group.

Part 3: Description of the Task

1. Distribute Handout 2. Briefly discuss the simple grammar and demonstrate the pronunciation of vowels and combination sounds.
2. Demonstrate a sentence or two, such as "Once upon a time, there were three little pigs . . ." or "Open the door or I'll blow your house in!"

Part 4: Piglish Practice

1. Tell the group to take the next few minutes to look over Handout 2 and to try out a few basics. Exhort them not to be afraid to practice the sounds and gestures—whispering, speaking out loud, gesturing, and such.
2. After the initial practice (7–10 minutes), stop the process and ask participants to reflect silently on how they are trying to learn the language. Suggest that they may continue their learning as they have been, or they may try another method: working with another person or even three or four people; writing the words out, talking out loud. . . .
3. Tell the group that as they continue to study, they should now put together several phrases as part of the story. (The time remaining should be 10–15 minutes.)

Part 5: Small-Group Practice

1. Form small groups of about three to six people (depending on the number of participants).
2. Tell the group you will assign a part of the story to each small group. Do this by walking by each group and indicating what part—the beginning, middle, or end of the story—they should work on.

3. Each group needs to work on their portion of the story, utilizing contributions from each person.

Part 6: Large-Group Report

1. Select one person from each group to tell a part of the story in turn. Do not worry if there is more than one group assigned to each part of the story.
2. Applaud everyone's efforts.

Part 7: Debriefing (Small Groups)

1. Ask the groups to use a flip chart to summarize their responses:
   - What was the most difficult thing about learning to communicate in a new language?
   - Describe the feelings you had while trying to speak and understand others.
   - How did these feelings affect your behavior?
2. One person from each group should summarize the answers and be prepared to give a brief response.

Part 8: Large-Group Discussion

1. Use some of the questions below to facilitate a discussion about this experience:
   - What are some examples of feelings identified in your group?
   - How did these feelings affect your individual and group behavior?
   - What were the hardest parts of learning this language?
   - How many of you used English (or another language's) words or pronunciation while trying to tell the story? Why would people do this?
   - What traits seemed to contribute to the most "successful" Piglish speaker?

   Note: The leader should mix in some observations of how people were attempting to learn the language. She might also ask the group how they observed others in the learning process. The leader should be aware that the level of enthusiasm she uses to introduce the exercise and encourage participants will have a direct impact on the manner in which the exercise is carried out. This should be recognized as similar to the way people approach the learning as well as how they use a new language in unfamiliar settings. In the course of discussion of the process questions, the participants should also develop insights about how the lack of language fluency and comprehension can limit and narrow the scope of one's functioning in the world. Encourage expressions of empathy and insight for how people might now regard those who do not speak English fluently. The questions below might also help with this discussion.

- How does it feel to communicate with someone who has limited understanding of your language?
- What kinds of things might happen if a person can only communicate at a very elementary level?

Part 9: Summary

1. Ask the participants what they have learned from this exercise, and how what they have learned may affect their behavior. Take as many examples as time permits.
2. Summarize major points and conclude with a few words in Piglish.

Caveats and Options

1. To use the activity as an opening ice breaker in a cross-cultural training setting, modify it in the following ways:
   - Use fewer questions.
   - Focus more on the feeling responses to the exercise.
   - Eliminate the small-group development of the story line (Part 5) and the small-group discussion (Part 7).
   - Modify the final questions so that you can make a smooth transition to the main portion of the training.
   - Shorten the time for practice.

   Or, if the activity is used as a team building exercise:
   - Organize the group into teams, assigning the task of making sure that everyone learns the language.
   - Or emphasize the shift to group work, asking the group to take on the task of making sure everyone learns some of the language.

- Add the following questions to the discussion:
  How did your group work together?
  Who took leadership roles for accomplishing the task?
  Were people who were accomplished in making the sounds and speaking Piglish recognized by the group?
  How did each person feel about his activity and role in the small group?
  How did this group activity compare with the individual work?
  Note: This last question may produce answers such as: "I worked more efficiently by myself . . . ." This should not lead to a discussion of how groups work or what effective group behavior is.
3. If used to explore language, culture, and world view, add questions such as:
   - Did the style of communicating or the topic of conversation (the story) affect how you felt about speaking Piglish? How?
   - Is there anything you wanted to say and could not? Did the amount of vocabulary limit the range of what you were able to express? Did it limit your thought processes or how you felt? If so, how?
   - Surely some personality traits manifested themselves during your Piglish-learning/speaking experience. Could any of those be considered cultural traits? For example: risk taking, perfectionism, affirmation or rejection of others according to ability levels, assumptions about talent, intelligence, values about verbal prowess, and so on? (Who got to tell the story from your group? Why? Might another culture [Piglers] have chosen another person?)
   - What assumptions did you make about Piglers based on their language and style of communication and vice versa?
   - Have the participants attempt to describe some of their feelings about language learning and learning Piglish in Piglish and process how different (more difficult?) it is to use the vocabulary in another context.

References and Further Reading

Lapinsky, T., & Hartley, C. (in press). Piglish: A language learning simulation. In S. M. Fowler (Ed.), *The intercultural sourcebook* (vol. 2). Yarmouth, ME: Intercultural Press.

Volunteers in Intercultural Programs, Youth for Understanding International Exchange. (1989). *Learning about language.* Intercultural Communication Series. Washington, DC: Author.

Appendix

Handout 1

The Story of the Three Little Pigs

Once upon a time, there were three little pigs who lived by a forest. They were very happy. One day they decided to build houses. One of the pigs built his house of straw. The second little pig built his house of sticks. The third pig built his house of bricks.

After the houses were finished, the pigs went to sleep, each in his own house. A big bad wolf came out of the forest and went to the house of straw.

"Little pig, little pig—let me in!" said the wolf.

The first pig said, "Not by the hair of my chinny-chin-chin."

The wolf said, "I'll huff and I'll puff and I'll blow your house down!"

So he huffed and puffed and blew the house of straw down. The pig ran to the house of his brother, in the house made of sticks.

The wolf went to the house of sticks next and shouted, "Little pigs, little pigs, let me in, or I'll blow this house down too!"

The two pigs were afraid, but they said, "Not by the hair of our chinny-chin-chins!"

So the wolf huffed and puffed, and huffed and puffed, and down went the house of sticks. The two little pigs ran to the brick house their brother pig had built. The wolf followed close behind.

"I know you're in there little pigs. Let me in, or I'll blow your house down."

While the two little pigs hid under the bed, the third pig stood in front of his door and said, "Not by the hair of my chinny-chin-chin, Wolf!"

With that, the wolf began to huff and puff, and he tried to blow down the brick house but nothing happened. The wolf huffed and puffed until he had to lie down to rest. Then he decided to get up onto the roof and try to go down the chimney. The third pig put a large pot of hot water in the fireplace and waited for the wolf.

The third pig heard the wolf on the roof as he tried to get down the chimney. Suddenly, with a big splash, the wolf fell down the chimney into the pot. Quickly, the third pig tied up the wet wolf and left him in the water.

The three little pigs were so happy, they danced around the room singing, "Who's afraid of the big bad wolf, the big bad wolf, the big bad wolf. Who's afraid of the big bad wolf, the big bad wolf—not I!"

Handout 2

Piglish: A Modern Language
Instructions and Vocabulary List

Introduction

Piglish is a modern language, and is derived from an island culture that was established when European settlers were shipwrecked with a load of swine destined for the New World in the 16th century. The survivors were mainly a group of children and 1,400 swine. The language was developed on the basis of the interactions between the swine and a 2-year-old human's command of English. Such notions as time and space also reflect a 2-year-old's perceptions.

You will be happy to know that both the children and the swine flourished together in the new society with their rudimentary language. The language and the culture have evolved over the years to a point where a fluent native speaker can meet all needs for survival. You must realize, of course, that fluent speakers use a great many gestures and nonverbal cues to make up for the lack of extensive vocabulary and complexity of language structure. Be careful about assumptions you might make about the limited world view of Piglers solely based on verbal competency.

Grammar

The vocabulary included here is enough to get you started in the language. The vocabulary is approximately what a 2-year-old, modern Pigler would know. The basic grammar of the language (word order to form sentences) follows English closely. For example, an ordinary sentence starts with a noun or pronoun (*pig, I*), followed by a verb (*am, is, are*), followed by an adjective (*hungry*). You will also notice that Piglish does not have separate pronouns for *I* or *we, you* or *they*. The island culture was very group (litter) oriented, and such distinctions are meaningless to a Pigler!

Verbs in Piglish have only a single tense, and gestures are used to indicate past, present and future. Verbs are not conjugated to agree with pronouns. For example, *I am happy* sounds the same as *We are happy*, and so do *You are happy, She is happy,* and *He is happy.* They are all said exactly alike. However, it will be perfectly clear in communication by pointing in different ways and squatting (or rising on the toes) at the right time, whether you are expressing a past, present, or future tense, as well as *I* or *we.*

Pronunciation

The language is quite phonetic and sounds like a guttural or grunted English. It follows the same consonant sounds of English, but the vowel sounds are only as follows:

a = ah, as in *father*	o = oh, as in *bone*
e = ay, as in *hay*	u = oo, as in *fool*
i = ee, as in *me*	

Special combination sounds are varieties of grunting sounds. Here are some examples:

mmmn = said with lips closed and in the throat, as in *mmmn good*

uug = said with the lips pursed in a round I, followed by a partial stop, as in *oo-ga*

nhhh = said with the mouth closed and through the nose with a grunting sound in a low tone

plddd = made bussing the tongue in the mouth in a soft flutter

puhbb = made by buzzing the lips the way a horse does

Gestures With Meaning

Finger points at the indicated person (*you, me, I, they, we*), accompanied by the generic pronoun for all persons, *uug*, pronounced *oo-ga.*

Squatting (used with verbs): indicates past tense; deep squat is long time ago; slight knee bend indicates yesterday or single past action.

Tip-toes (used with verbs): indicates the future tense.

Eyes wide open or eyes closed: indicates degree or emphasis such as when an English speaker would use -er on the end of a word (*bigger*).

The negative can be formed by crossing the forearms across the chest as the verb is spoken.

Verbs

to go =	mnnph	to dance =	sqo
to be (is, are, am) =	uugh	to get (up/down) =	blugh*
to laugh =	snuff-snuff	to bind/tie =	sbynog
to look/see =	ibah	to wait =	tiple-pldddd
to let/allow =	huuba	to huff/puff =	ugh-puhbbb
to blow =	whiff	to say =	ilk-eh
to live =	nnh-bah	to run =	mo-mo
to open =	uudle-uuh	to leave =	bibi
to sit =	chachu	to sing =	ugh-lala
to put =	di-shy	to finish =	nnb-fi
to build =	batuu		

*gesture up or down as appropriate

Nouns

pigs =	uugi	home/house =	sty
food =	mmmn	wolf =	groof
bricks =	baaba	straw =	hesi
sticks =	waawa	road/trail =	longa
thing =	daa	door =	puhbbb-ah
minutes =	snips	time =	snip-snip
hair =	mope	chin =	chuga
roof =	topah	fireplace =	waa-daa
pot =	daa-ruh	forest =	nhh-waa
water =	mot-ve	splash =	mot-whiff
chimney =	waa-buh		

Adjectives, Adverbs, Prepositions, and Conjunctions

big =	enorpub	bad =	yuk
good =	slurp	happy =	squil
scared =	trull	stupid =	owe
not/no =	nabb	and =	muucha
or =	da	down =	flak
of =	di	once =	uber
the =	der	in =	tut
little =	squiz	hungry =	supcha
upon =	squa	wet =	move

Numbers (same for first, second)

1 = pee		4 = pee sno	
2 = pee pee		5 = sno	
3 = pee pee pee		6 = sno pee	

Commonly Used Expressions

Open the door =	Uudle=uuh der puhbbb-ah
I'm hungry =	Uug supcha (pointing to stomach)
Once upon a time =	Uber squa snip-snip (squatting down)
There were =	Cog (squatting down)
Let me in =	Huba uug tut
Who's afraid =	Uug trull

Contributor

Judith M. Blohm, formerly a classroom teacher in California, Virginia, and Liberia, West Africa, is currently a consultant in instructional design, writing and editing, and training for children, youth, and adults preparing for living and working in multicultural settings. She is also on the Governing Council of SIETAR International.

Man From Mars: Unspoken Assumptions of Words*

Levels
Beginning +

Aims
Discover that words
alone may not convey
complete messages
Explore some of the
assumptions that the
exercise exposes and
the relevance of non-
verbal communication
Consider the inter-
relationships between
language, culture, and
world view
Develop skills in
speaking more clearly
and precisely when
communicating with
someone speaking a
second/foreign language

Class Time
30 minutes +

Preparation Time
30 minutes

Resources
Pack of cigarettes and
small box (preferably)
or book of matches

The exercise is used to demonstrate that communication is more than learning to pronounce and use words and grammar. The specific lesson of this exercise is that words carry unspoken assumptions that must also be learned in order to communicate effectively across cultures. This is because assumptions are learned as culture is transmitted. Assumptions—or unspoken meanings—are internalized as one is socialized and educated by society and therefore must be brought to awareness. This activity helps do that.

The creator of this exercise is unknown. I first learned about and used it in Peace Corps training programs in southern Africa in the early 1970s.

Procedure

Part 1: Introduction

1. Brief the student role playing the person from Mars so that he or she can practice the role before beginning the exercise. The role is to take all instructions literally and not interpret anything. This is difficult on two levels: The student has to unlearn natural reactions plus keep a straight face.

   Examples of instructions and behaviors:
   - *come in*: walk straight into room and continue walking into anything in the way (people, chairs, wall) until told to stop

---

*This exercise originally appeared in *Introduction to Cross-Cultural Communication,* by Judith Blohm, 1991. Washington, DC: Youth for Understanding International Exchange. Reprinted with permission. Copyright © Youth for Understanding, Washington, DC.

- *turn around:* continue turning until told to stop
- *sit down:* immediately sit wherever one is: on the floor, on someone's lap, on a chair
- *pick up:* grasp strongly with hand and lift; that is, do not think whether it should be held upright or picked up gently unless told to do so
- *put ___ in your mouth:* stuff it in, whole, unless instructed more specifically

2. Tell participants that they are going to meet a visitor, a man or woman from Mars, in a few minutes. This person has studied English from a book but has never really used it. They are to invite the person in, and have her sit down and light a cigarette. (Because fewer people smoke now than in the past, the trainer should be sure a pack of cigarettes and box of matches are available.)

Part 2: The Exercise

1. Go to the door and inform the "Martian" (who is outside the room) that he or she should knock in about a minute and then follow instructions.
2. When the Martian knocks, let the participants take over. You or the facilitator should observe but not intervene until the Martian has lit a cigarette.
3. If time must be limited, have someone go to door and escort the Martian to a seat near the cigarettes and matches. Just getting the person to that point could take more than 5 minutes.

Part 3: Debriefing

1. Ask the participants to describe what happened.
2. Ask the participants how they used information they learned early in their encounter with the Martian to improve later communication. If they did not, ask why not.
3. Explore reasons why the Martian may have acted as he or she did (e.g., sat on the floor, burned finger with the match).

4. Explore some different assumptions behind common daily activities; ask participants for personal experiences with other cultures. Examples are behaviors that accompany verbal greetings (and if different, by gender, age, status), or how one interprets what "being on time" means if the stated time is for a doctor's appointment, an informal dinner with friends, or a party, for example.

5. Ask when and how we learn the assumptions that we have—for example, how to pick up different types of objects without having to be told specifically each time. (Children are taught the nuances as they learn to follow directions and speak. Think about how one must correct children when they first pick up a cat or a glass of milk.)

Part 4: Application and Summary

1. Summarize and apply learning appropriate to participants and purposes for the use of the exercise. For example, if participants work with second or foreign language speakers, discuss how they can make communication clearer and what they should expect in terms of inappropriate responses/behaviors that often accompany the use of a second language.

Caveats and Options

1. If the activity is used to train persons working with second/foreign language speakers, you may want to add the following discussion questions or prompts:

   ● Why didn't the Martian ask questions? (perhaps shy, embarrassed; never had spoken with anyone; overwhelmed just trying to listen and do as told)

   ● Replay the exercise (changing the task the Martian is asked to perform), allowing the Martian limited responses and question asking. (In keeping with the Martian's lack of experience with the use of the language, have the Martian only ask very rudimentary questions, such as How? Where? What is a _____?, using them inappropriately sometimes, misunderstanding the answer, continuing inappropriate behavior in some cases.

   ● Add debrief of second activity.

- In what ways was the second round different?
- How did the Martian feel?
- How did participants feel about their interactions? Did they develop any feelings about this Martian or Martian culture in general?

2. If the activity is used to explore interrelationships between language, culture, and world view, add the following questions:

- Would any assumptions have differed if the "person from Mars" had been of the opposite sex? If the facilitator had been? Ask both of them (and the participants) how they felt about the exercise and what impact language had on their feelings.
- Why do we always say *man* from Mars? How might the use of the generic form *man* to mean humankind influence our assumptions?
- What is the significance of the imperative (command) form in this exercise? What would happen if you said "please" before each command? What type of relationship between speakers is implied by the imperative form?

3. If the activity is used to explore more deeply assumptions of language and behaviors that accompany it, include the following.

- Follow this exercise with a cross-cultural simulation, such as Zeezoos and Yahoos (see Fantini et al., 1984) or Bafá Bafá (see Shirts, 1973). Include in the debriefing discussion of the specific clues that mislead participants because of the assumed meanings in their culture (e.g., women are inferior in Zeezoos and Yahoos because of their behavior in relation to the man; trying to figure out the other culture in Bafá Bafá by interpreting through the values in one's own culture).

4. If the activity is used with children or youth:

- Replace the lighting of a cigarette with a different, but similarly complicated task, such as making and eating a peanut butter and jelly sandwich. (See "Operations" by Fantini in this volume.)

References and Further Reading

Blohm, J. (1991). *Introduction to cross-cultural communication.* Washington, DC: Youth for Understanding International Exchange.

Fantini, A. E. et al. (1984). The Zeezoos and the Yahoos. In *Cross-cultural orientation: A guide for leaders and educators* (pp. 29–31). Brattleboro, VT: The Experiment Press.

Shirts, R. G. (1973). *Bafá Bafá—A cross-cultural simulation.* La Jolla, CA: Simile II.

Contributor

Judith M. Blohm, formerly a classroom teacher in California, Virginia, and Liberia, West Africa, is currently a consultant in instructional design; writing and editing; and training for children, youth, and adults preparing for living and working in multicultural settings. She is also on the governing council of SIETAR International.

The Cocktail Party: Exploring Nonverbal Communication*

Level
Intermediate +

Aims
Talk with people who exhibit different nonverbal behaviors from one's own
Analyze the feelings those behaviors produce and ascribe corresponding attributes
Consider nonverbal behaviors as a part of the whole communication process, with the strong potential for unconscious miscommunication in a new cultural setting
Explore relationships between nonverbal language, culture, and world view

Class Time
30 minutes–1 hour

Preparation Time
15 minutes

Resources
Written instructions regarding five nonverbal behaviors need to be selected
Blank flip charts

This exercise is designed to help people experience the effects of nonverbal behaviors. It may be used for various purposes. For example, it might be used as a nonthreatening experiential introduction to cross-cultural encounters, as one segment of a larger unit on cross-cultural communication, or as an example of one of the dimensions of communication.

In the format presented here, I used the exercise to introduce a unit on communicating across cultures for U.S. adults working with foreign students on the Youth for Understanding International Exchange program. The specific behaviors used are not common in the United States.

Procedure

Part 1: Introduction

1. Tell the group that they are going to have the opportunity to discuss the question presented on the flip chart for about 5 minutes. Reveal a simple, but relevant question to the group, such as "What do you think of this room/building as a training site?"
2. Indicate that they will each have a particular item to keep in mind during the discussion and that you will distribute this information via slips of paper.
3. Have them divide themselves into stand-up groups of five, and as they do so, hand out an individual slip of paper containing a nonverbal behavior to each person in each group (see Appendix).
4. Do not give participants a lot of time to worry about the instructions or answer questions. Move them quickly into the activity.

---

*This exercise originally appeared in *Introduction to Cross-Cultural Communication,* by Judith Blohm, 1991. Washington, DC: Youth for Understanding International Exchange. Reprinted with permission. Copyright © Youth for Understanding, Washington, DC.

Part 2: Small-Group Discussions

1. Encourage groups to start talking, even if you need to walk up and ask someone to start.
2. Move about and observe what is happening. It is likely that participants will feel embarrassed or uncomfortable doing some of the behaviors as well as having someone else touch them or get too close. There may be laughter.

Part 3: Large-Group Debriefing

1. Ask group to reassemble.
2. Use a flip chart to record their descriptions of how others in their group behaved. Begin with descriptions, saving reactions until all descriptions are listed. It may be difficult to get behaviors; they are most likely to say that someone was weird or disruptive and so on.

What People Did	*How I Felt/Reacted*
Touched	
Looked down, away	
Stood too close	
Jumped in before others	
Finished speaking	
Snapped fingers to get attention	

3. After the ways people behaved are listed, go back over the list and solicit reactions. (You can solicit reactions to/feelings about each action or make a general list.) The lists may look like this:

What People Did	*How I Felt/Reacted*
Touched	Uncomfortable
Looked down, away	Confused
Stood too close	Annoyed
Jumped in before others finished	Attacked
Speaking	Angry
Snapped fingers	Disregarded
	Felt lied to

4. Communication includes more than words; what people do—their nonverbal behaviors—also conveys messages. What are some of the attributes that nonverbal behaviors may convey? List them on a flip chart. Examples may include character judgments (e.g., rude, aggressive, strange, weird) or politeness/education (e.g., uneducated, bad manners, disrespectful).

5. Rather than making the attributions, consider other ways of understanding different nonverbal behaviors. On a second flip chart, put up the following additional columns and explore answers (such as the examples given below).

Possible Significance (Values)	*Why*
warmth vs. intimacy	social custom
respect/deference vs. honesty	history
interest/involvement vs. rudeness	honor
status/hierarchy vs. equality	geography, climate
	position, class

6. Identify some nonverbal behaviors common to the group. Ask them all to demonstrate (without words) that they are angry, bored, or disapproving or that someone else is crazy. Discuss when and how they learned to display such behaviors. If there are variations in nonverbal behaviors known and used by people in the group, explore their origins.

7. Some nonverbal behaviors different from your own patterns may just seem strange. Others will convey very negative reactions. All of them will probably be somewhat annoying and/or detract from communication.

Part 4: Summary

1. Ask the participants what they learned from this exercise. One of the points they should have learned is that to communicate with someone else fully, one must share the same understanding on nonverbal behaviors. Clearly, this is a potential problem area in cross-cultural situations.

Caveats and Options

This exercise may be used for various purposes. For example, it might be used as a nonthreatening experiential introduction to cross-cultural encounters, as one segment of a larger unit on cross-cultural communication, or as an example of one of the dimensions of communication. For ESOL students, it could help them focus on and learn nonverbal behaviors used by English speakers. Here are some ways to adapt the exercises for other uses:

1. If used with non-U.S. participants or a mixed group:
   - Select nonverbal behaviors not common to the participants, or with enough variety that everyone in the group will experience at least one that is different.
2. If used as an opening to general cross-cultural awareness training
   - Pursue further the feeling level and attributes.
   - Discuss other types of cultural differences.
   - Explore reasons for cultural differences.
   - Explore the longer-term effects of cultural difference: ability to perform job satisfactorily and use role-appropriate behaviors, causes and manifestations of culture stress, and so on.
   - Develop strategies for dealing with differences, depending on the group and its needs.
3. If used with a focus on cross-cultural communication
   - Explore communication expressed through words, tone, and nonverbal cues.
   - Beginning with the examples in the exercise, explore proxemics, oculesics, kinesics, haptics, and chronemics.
   - Other?
4. If used with younger students
   - Change the setting to a meeting by their lockers, in the cafeteria, or at the school bus stop.
   - Change the discussion to something more relevant to the age group.

Reference

Blohm, J. (1991). *Introduction to cross-cultural communication.* Washington, DC: Youth for Understanding International Exchange.

Appendix

Handout: Exploring Nonverbal Communication

Make one copy of this handout for each group of four or five participants. Cut the phrases apart and place a set of the different behaviors in an envelope for each group, to be distributed during the exercise.

- Do not look directly into the eyes of the speaker. Either look past them or drop your gaze to the floor.

- Stand closer than is comfortable to people in the group, especially when you are speaking (i.e., take a step closer to the person you are addressing than you normally would).

- Touch people on the arm or shoulder as you speak.

- Jump in before other speakers have finished sentences to add your own points.

- Raise your arm and snap your fingers to get attention, to be recognized to speak.

Contributor

Judith M. Blohm, formerly a classroom teacher in California, Virginia, and Liberia, is currently a consultant in instructional design; writing and editing; and training for children, youth, and adults preparing for living and working in multicultural settings. She is also on the governing council of SIETAR International.

Talking Rocks: A Simulation on the Origins of Writing*

*This exercise is adapted and reprinted with permission of the originator, Robert F. Vernon. Portions of the activity are copyrighted by Simulation Training Systems.

Levels
Any

Aims
Understand how writing as a form of communication may have evolved and some essential elements needed in making up a writing system
Experience and use the basic parts of speech, grammar, and syntax
Challenge students to experience decision making with insufficient data
Develop an image of prehistoric or nonliterate peoples that is more complex, sophisticated, and empathetic than conventional stereotypes

Class Time
2-3 hours

Preparation Time
5-10 minutes

Resources
Survival messages
Large sheets of unlined newsprint and felt marker pens
One easel/group
Scratch paper

Talking Rocks is designed for pupils from Grades 5-8, but may be used by high school and college groups studying literature, grammar and sentence structure, communications, anthropology, ethnography, linguistics, and art. It promotes use of a second language when used in the context of a language class.

All players in this activity are members of the Eagle People, a nomadic tribe of shepherds who must travel in search of new pastures. The Eagle People do not all live together. Bands of Eagle People communicate with each other by leaving messages near their campsites—messages that contain vital instructions for survival. Each band or group must encode their message into a pictograph without the use of modern symbols, letters, or numbers. What often evolves is a creative communication system. What happens along the way is a lot of brainstorming, cooperation, and team building within the groups.

Procedure

1. Before beginning the simulation, arrange the overall area by creating spaces that isolate each group as much as possible. Arrange the spaces so that the content of the survival messages will not inadvertently be discovered. When available, use room dividers, chalkboards on rollers, and so on. If you are playing in an average sized classroom with about 30 students, you could divide them into six groups of 5 students and use the six easels to separate the groups.

2. Divide students into groups or bands and assign an easel to each group. There should be no more than 5 students in a band. If there were 29 students in a classroom, for example, they could be divided into five bands of 5 students each and one band of 4. If there were only 15 persons in the class, they could be divided into five bands of 3 students each. Keep groups as small as possible to ensure that everyone can participate.

3. Begin by developing the Eagle culture. Tell the participants that they are going to become Eagle People and write Eagle messages to one another without using words or modern symbols. Tell them that their goal should be to survive as long as possible and that there can be no talking between groups. You should say something like the following:

> You are the Eagle People, a great nation made up of small groups of families who live together in bands. You all speak the same language and share the same customs and traditions. You have flocks of sheep and goats that give you meat and milk for nourishment, leather and wool for clothes, moccasins, rope, and blankets. Each band of Eagle People lives apart from every other band and is separated by a journey of many days over high plateaus and arid deserts. You help each other whenever you can. When you move your campsites, you leave helpful messages behind for the next band of Eagle People who camp there. You do this by carving the messages onto large flat rocks [point to the easels] with stone tools [hold up a marker pen].

4. Hand out one survival message to each band. As you are doing this, remind them of the three important rules:
   - use only pictures—no modern symbols
   - do not share the message with any other band in the room
   - do not talk to any other band

5. Tell them how long they have to develop their message for those who follow them. Usually 7–10 minutes is enough. While they are developing their drawing, circulate and act as a timekeeper. It is important to get them working on their task as soon as possible, but refrain from giving advice and suggestions. If one group completes

the survival picture much faster than the others, have the members try a second version and select the best of the two. Each group should be made to feel responsible for its own survival.

6. Give a 3-minute warning when the best (or only) pictures emerge. Generally the first round takes a bit longer than subsequent rounds.

7. Call time. Collect the written survival messages so that unauthorized people won't see them. Tell each band to move to the next campsite, taking their personal possessions with them but leaving their drawings behind. Once they arrive at their new site, tell them it is important for their survival to interpret the pictograph left by the preceding group. Give them 5-7 minutes to do this. You might say

> You have just migrated into a new territory. The trek was long and hard, over many miles of burning desert. You are very tired and hungry. If you do not find food and water for yourself and your flocks, you are going to be in deep trouble. Nearby is a message chiseled on a cliff. You must figure out what it means. Remember that this message is important for your survival, so be careful in deciding exactly what it means.

8. After 5-7 minutes, call time and evaluate whether or not the groups have correctly interpreted the picture's message. You are the sole judge in this. Each interpretation must include a survival element, such as "poisoned water"; a sense of direction, such as "go east"; and a sense of time and distance, such as "a half day's journey."

9. Announce which groups have correctly interpreted the pictures and can continue to play and which groups misinterpreted the message and have died out. It is impractical and undesirable to have dead groups with nothing to do. There are several alternatives:
   - allow each group a second chance
   - if only one group dies, have members assist you
   - assign specific observer tasks that will help during the discussion, such as observing the patterns of work in the successful groups, group leadership patterns, the evolution of symbols
   - have dead groups join living groups as ghosts or ancestral spirits; have spirits consult with the living

10. Hand out a new survival message to each group and proceed as before. Repeat these rounds as long as you have time and continued interest. Typically there will be three or four rounds. This game can continue during the same class period over several days. Collect the materials and instruct the groups to re-form at the next class meeting. Four rounds usually take about 2 hours, and a third hour should be devoted to analysis.

11. Conduct a discussion analyzing the experience. If appropriate, begin with questions for a small-group discussion. For example, ask the groups to recall a specific experience that happened in the game that is immediately applicable and relevant to the learning objectives. Have them identify the key elements that contributed to the experience or event. Have the group analyze what happened. Why did the event happen the way that it did? What roles did the key elements play? Have the group generalize from the analysis to other similar events. Have them draw conclusions about the event based on their analysis. In the large-group discussion, you might ask them what tribal people were really like. Competitive? Cooperative? Both? When? Where? How? Why? You can ask about our common stereotypes of tribal people. Ask what the similarities and differences are between the writing system that evolved during the game and the English writing system. Which survival techniques worked? Which did not work? How did they communicate within their groups? Did leaders develop? How did it feel to be an ancestral spirit? How did the group members relate to their ancestral spirits?

12. Conclude by putting people back into their original bands. Ask them to complete this list: Anyone playing this game will likely come to the following conclusions. (Example: It is hard to write messages about time.) Have them come up with a list of 5–10 conclusions. Then have them rank their conclusions for importance. Discuss these in the large group.

Caveats and Options

1. With very young children, try a practice run and take a group through a round of play using local scenarios such as "go to the north fence on the playground."

2. Depending on language proficiency, it may be necessary to review the vocabulary in the scenarios prior to playing.
3. For adults and older children, you can add religious, art, and hunting magic messages to the survival messages to make the game more difficult for them and for you. The value of this variation is that it helps students realize that petroglyphs and pictographs were probably drawn for a variety of reasons and that interpreting them is extremely difficult when the motive behind the drawing is not known.
4. Acquire a teacher's manual: It is available for $15 from Simulation Training Systems (formerly Simile II), Box 910, Del Mar, CA 92014 USA; tel 619-755-0272. Although you could run this simulation game from the description given here, it is well worth the cost of the teacher's manual to have the survival messages, a checklist for running the simulation, additional uses for the game, a more in-depth description of the Eagle People, suggestions for religious and hunt magic messages, and more detailed questions for the discussion.

References and Further Reading

Fowler, S. M., & Mumford, M. G. (Eds.). (1995). *Intercultural sourcebook: Cross-cultural training methods.* Yarmouth, ME: Intercultural Press.

Vernon, R. F. (1978). *Talking rocks: A simulation on the origins of writing.* Del Mar, CA: Simile II.

Contributor

Sandra M. Fowler, formerly president of SIETAR International and member of the North American Simulation and Gaming Association, is an intercultural specialist in Washington, DC.

Part III: Activities for Sociolinguistic Exploration

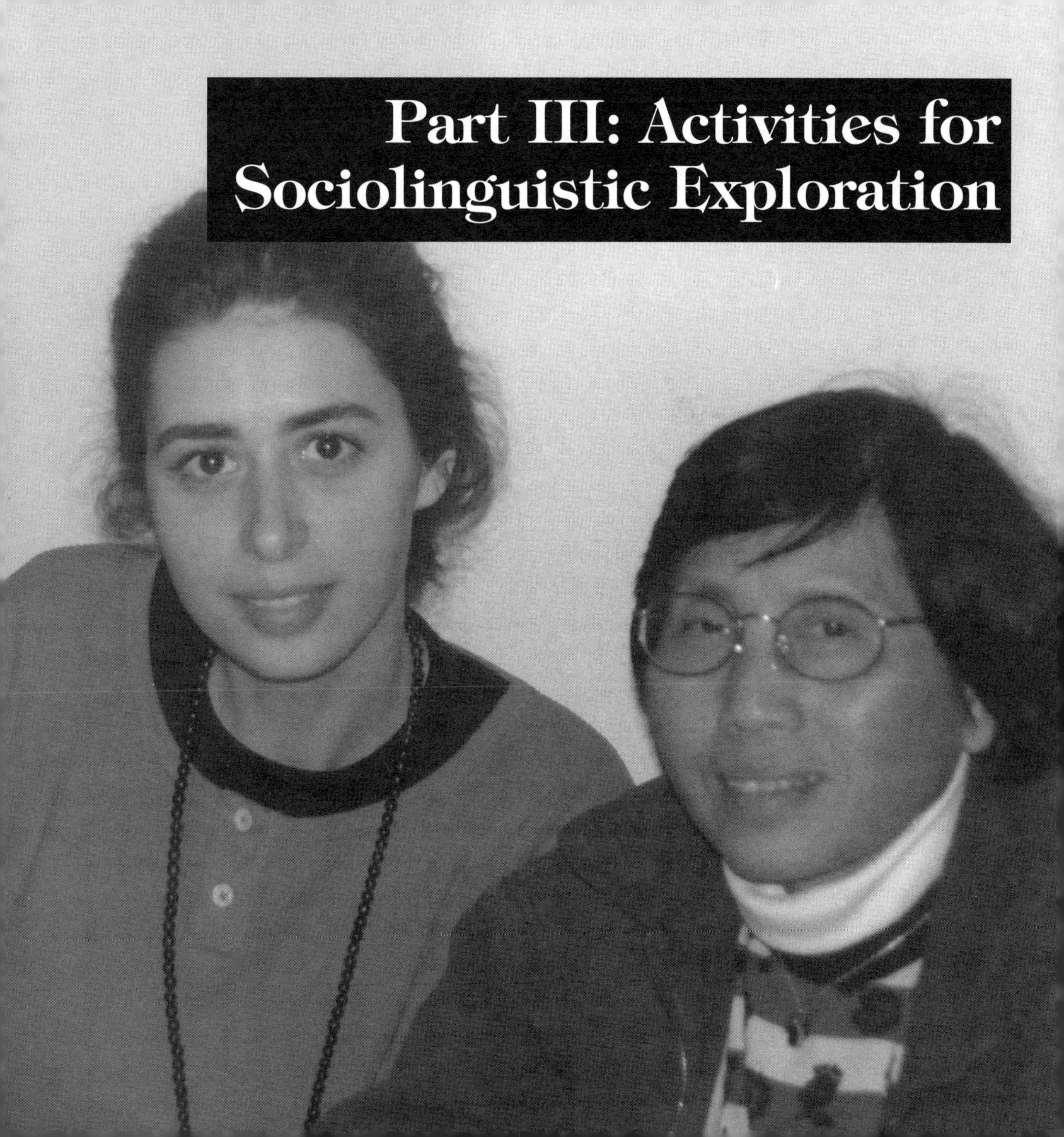

A Sociocultural Matrix

Levels
Intermediate +

Aims
Learn different styles of
language expression
appropriate for varying
contexts
Explore social factors
that determine the need
for each style
Understand the
connection between
social context and
language expression and
the variety of speech
styles used by native
speakers of English

Class Time
30 minutes

Preparation Time
30 minutes

A sociocultural matrix can serve as an important aid to the teacher interested in helping learners develop an understanding of and an ability to communicate both effectively (as judged by the student; i.e., an etic view) and appropriately (as judged by the hosts; i.e., an emic view). Both are important for intercultural communication. Exploration of language expression and its relationship to social context, in fact, is an important dimension of developing intercultural competence and can serve to foster the various speech styles learners will need for interacting with English speakers.

Procedure

1. Ask students about situations in which they find themselves on a daily basis, for example, in school, in the cafeteria, on the street, on a bus (or, if time is limited, give them a ready-made list that you have prepared in advance). Then have them identify some people they often encounter in these situations (e.g., waiter, police, teacher) and aspects of those people (e.g., young or old, friends, strangers, waiters).

2. On a flip chart, or on a photocopied matrix, list situations down the left-hand column and the people and/or their attributes across the top (see sample in the Appendix). Then have students create a list of tasks.

3. In pairs, have students choose various items from the grid and role play the tasks as time permits, checking off the ones they do.

4. At the end of the allotted time, have the class come back together to discuss some of the ways they changed their language expression (e.g., courtesy expressions, modals) and the reasons for this. Discuss what some important sociocultural factors relevant to the target

culture are and how these affect styles of speech. Have students compare and contrast these with factors in their own culture(s).

5. Note any special questions or language needs that may arise so that you can modify how you present future lessons.

Caveats and Options

1. Vary situations, contextual features, and tasks in accordance with learner needs. For example, younger learners and students will obviously have different sociocultural needs from those of older learners in a multinational organization.
2. If time permits, have students role play situations in front of the class. Have others note whether the language and interaction were appropriate for the situation and task.
3. For homework, have students collect other situations and variables for use in future classes. They may also identify and record language styles used in each situation observed.
4. Include sociocultural exploration and practice as an ongoing part of the course.

Appendix

Handout 1: A Sample Sociocultural Matrix

Interlocutors:	Friend	Teacher	Waiter	Police	Bus Driver
Variables:	Older	Stranger	Male	Female	Authority
Situations:					
Classroom					
Cafeteria					
Street					
Bus					

Handout 2: Some Possible Tasks

1. Introduce a friend to the class.
2. Ask the school nurse for some aspirin.
3. Request directions from someone on the street.
4. Return an unwanted item to a store with a receipt (or without a receipt).
5. You witnessed an accident and wish to inform the police.
6. You bumped into an elderly woman on the bus and wish to apologize.
7. You pick up clothes at the cleaner and discover that a shirt was torn.
8. You have a reservation on a flight but are told the flight is oversold.

Now create some of your own:

1. _____

2. _____

3. _____

4. _____

5. _____

6. _____

Contributor

Alvino E. Fantini, senior faculty member at the School for International Training, Brattleboro, Vermont, in the United States, is a past president of SIETAR International (Society for Intercultural Education, Training, and Research) and an international consultant on matters of language and intercultural communication.

Oops! There I Go Again

Levels
Any

Aims
Identify inappropriate
language use in an
intercultural situation
Suggest reasons they are
considered
inappropriate

Class Time
20–30 minutes

Preparation Time
15 minutes

Resources
5-minute segment of a
conversation recorded
on audiotape
Worksheets

This activity seeks to heighten the students' awareness of what is considered inappropriate in the target language and help them avoid or cope with such situations in their own dealings in that language.

Procedure

1. Introduce the activity briefly, explaining that the students should look out for gaffes, faux pas, inappropriate comments, questions, and reactions.
2. Play the segment of a conversation containing a number of inappropriate features. Students listen and make mental notes.
3. Distribute the worksheet. Play the segment again and this time have the students write down their observations and classify them on the chart.
4. In pairs or in small groups, have the students compare notes and discuss what they identified as inappropriate. They should try to draw up an agreed-upon list of gaffes. You may want to play the tape a third time as a final check before the agreed-upon list is presented.
5. Elicit a consensus list of the inappropriate features from the pairs/groups.
6. In pairs or groups, have the students discuss why such language use is considered inappropriate and make notes on the chart. Class discussion of their reasoning follows.

Caveats and Options

1. Make this activity easier by supplying beginners with a list of the inappropriate language, out of sequence, and asking them to number the faux pas according to the order in which they hear them.
2. Ask advanced students to rate the language according to the seriousness of the inappropriateness (minor slip to grievous gaffe).

96

3. Use a video segment. Both spoken and body language could then be observed.
4. Offer reinforcement by comparing other 5-minute segments or by focusing on one type of inappropriateness (e.g., topic or reaction) in each conversation.
5. Ask more advanced students to make conversations using role cards, with their classmates observing and discussing the appropriateness or otherwise of the interaction.
6. Have students compare what is considered inappropriate in the target language and culture with what is considered inappropriate in their own.

Appendix: Worksheet for Oops! There I Go Again

Listen to the conversation and note briefly what you consider inappropriate.

Classify the inappropriate features and fill in the chart.

WHY?

TOPIC   _____   _____

               _____   _____

COMMENT   _____   _____

               _____   _____

RESPONSE   _____   _____

               _____   _____

LENGTH	_____	_____
	_____	_____
TOPIC	_____	_____
CHANGE	_____	_____
	_____	_____

Contributor

Geraldine Hetherton is an EFL lecturer at Fukui Prefectural University in Matsuoka-cho, Fukui-Ken, Japan. She has also taught in Europe, Africa, and the Middle East.

What Shall I Call You?

Levels
Intermediate +

Aims
Learn to recognize
patterns in language use
Realize the connection
between language use
and cultural values

Class Time
1 hour

Preparation Time
15 minutes

Resources
None

The choices speakers make when using a language reveal much about their individual personalities as well as their culture's expectations. This activity focuses students' attention on the cultural reasons guiding their use of address forms.

Procedure

1. Ask students to divide a sheet of paper into three vertical columns and to number each column from 1 to 20.
2. Ask students to list in the first column the full names of 20 people they know.
3. Ask students to identify each of these people by writing their relationship to the student in the second column.
4. Ask students to imagine that each of the 20 people they have listed is walking one by one ahead of them in a shopping mall or on the street. In the third column, have students write the form they would use to get the attention of each of these people.
5. Have students examine their three columns looking for a pattern in their use of address forms. With which people do they use the same address form?
6. Have students classify the people on their list by forms of address.
7. Ask students to identify the reasons for their choices of address form. Students may identify age, occupation, length of time in contact, and nature of relationship, among their reasons.
8. Ask students to consider whether their system of address form usage is unique or reflective of their culture.
9. If their system of address form usage is culturally triggered, ask students to discuss what the system reveals about their culture.

Caveats and Options

1. Be sure that students' lists reflect a variety of relationships, so their lists have a variety of address forms.

References and Further Reading

Chan, D., Kaplan-Weinger, J., & Sandstrom, D. (1995). *Journeys to cultural understanding*. Boston: Heinle & Heinle.

Contributors

Deborah Sandstrom, Judith Kaplan-Weinger, and Debra Chan are university educators in linguistics and TESL, Sandstrom at the University of Illinois at Chicago, and Kaplan-Weinger and Chan at Northeastern Illinois University, also in Chicago, in the United States.

Exploring Relationships in Conversations

Levels
Intermediate +

Aim
Increase understanding
of the different speaking
styles English speakers
employ

Class Time
30 minutes–1 hour

Preparation Time
20 minutes

Resources
Copies of a set of short
dialogues for analysis

S tudents may need help in learning to recognize the subtle meanings within speaker relationships. The purpose of this activity is to examine how speakers adjust their speech styles according to differing social situations.

Procedure

1. Distribute copies of prepared dialogues to each student. Then, ask students to work in pairs to discuss them. Give students time to explore their understanding of the dialogue.
2. Provide brief explanations for any unfamiliar phrasing or vocabulary. Whenever possible, solicit student explanations.
3. Check for general comprehension of each dialogue without explaining the subtleties of the interactions between speakers.
4. Have students discuss each dialogue and then:
   - describe the relationship between the speakers in each dialogue
   - explain the purpose of the exchange between each pair of speakers in Dialogues A and B
   - tell how the relationship between the speakers changes the speech style of each speaker
   - describe the speech style of each set of speakers
   - determine if the communication was successful
   - identify the meaning of the underlined language expressions
   - in Dialogue A, lines l_3, l_7, l_8, & l_{10}, and Dialogue B, lines l_6, l_8, l_{11}, & l_{13}, identify what is understood by both speakers in each dialogue but is not expressed

Caveats and Options

1. Be as creative as possible. The extent to which students can discuss the nuances of the different speech styles will depend greatly on their language proficiency.
2. Have students work in pairs to create two short dialogues, one between two friends, and a second between a student and a teacher. Allow them to use the distributed dialogues as models.

Appendix

Handout 1

Dialogue A: Phil calls José to make plans to see a movie

l_1	J:	Hello.
l_2	P:	Hey, <u>what's up</u>? It's Phil.
l_3	J:	<u>What's doing</u>? Just got back from <u>working out</u>.
l_4	P:	<u>That's outstanding</u>. You're sure <u>in shape</u>. <u>Wanna go</u> to the
l_5		movies with Jan and me? There's a new Mel Gibson movie
l_6		I <u>wanna see</u>. What do <u>ya</u> think?
l_7	J:	<u>Yeah</u>, me too.
l_8	P:	Great! <u>Let's catch</u> the 3 o'clock show at the 86th Street
l_9		Quad. Okay?
l_{10}	J:	My brother wants to see it too. <u>I'll get him</u>.
l_{11}	P:	Think there'll be a problem with 3 o'clock?
l_{12}	J:	Nah. He's just taking it easy today.
l_{13}	P:	Cool. We <u>haven't seen</u> Tomás in a while. See <u>ya</u> then?
l_{14}	J:	Terrific!

Handout 2

Dialogue B: Rosita is speaking with Mrs. Balev of the lost and found department of Olympic Mall. Rosita is checking to see if her lost sweater <u>turned up.</u>

l_1 B: Hello, <u>may</u> I help you?

l_2 R: Yes, thanks. I was shopping at the Gap yesterday and <u>I lost</u>
l_3 <u>my sweater</u>.

l_4 B: Can you describe it?

l_5 R: Well, it's beige with small and large red flowers.

l_6 B: Wait a minute. I'll <u>check</u> what came in last night.

l_7 R: I hope you can find it. It's my favorite sweater.

l_8 B: [Mrs. Balev returns after a few minutes.] Yes, I think <u>we</u>
       <u>have something here</u>. What's your size?

l_9 R: <u>I'm a medium</u>. [pointing] Yes, that's my sweater. <u>Terrific</u>.

l_{10} B: We just need you <u>to sign for it</u>.

l_{11} R: Thanks. I couldn't sleep last night. I was so worried.

l_{12} B: Glad we could be of help to you! <u>Have a nice day</u>.

l_{13} R: <u>You too</u>.

Contributor

Virginia M. Tong is assistant professor of education at Hunter College of the City University of New York, where she teaches Methodology of TESOL and Introduction to Linguistics. Her research interests include acculturation and sociolinguistics.

Choosing (or Avoiding) Topics During a Conversation

Levels
Any

Aims
Recognize that cultural
differences should be
considered when
choosing a topic for a
conversation with native
speakers

Class Time
50 minutes

Preparation Time
1 hour

Resources
Dialogue with features
that students can
identify and contrast
with their own cultures

This activity offers the learner an opportunity to recognize and practice various conversation topics that are considered sociolinguistically delicate and best avoided. It also offers practice with the notions and functions of the target language.

Procedure

1. Ask the students culture-eliciting questions such as:
   - Within your own culture when you do not know someone well, what kinds of topics do you choose to discuss?
   - What would you not discuss?
   - Which topics have you found that people from other cultures or countries commonly use to initiate conversations with you? How do you feel about these choices?
   - What would you do if a person from another culture began discussing with you a topic that made you feel uncomfortable or that you did not want to talk about?
2. Have the students form small groups (three to four students).
3. Give each group a copy of a prepared cultural topic dialogue (see Appendix).
4. Ask the groups to read the dialogue and discuss cultural analysis points such as the following:
   - Find expressions that the native English speaker exaggerated in order to emphasize her point.
   - What question did the second language student ask that the native speaker did not answer? Why do you think an answer was refused?
   - Why do you think Brandy ended the conversation so quickly? What was her impression of Kim?

- How did Kim feel? What is her impression of Brandy now?
- What can you deduce about the culture of the United States from this dialogue?

5. Guide a class discussion concerning the answers the different groups found.
6. Ask students to express ideas about how this conversation would change if it had occurred in their native culture(s).

Caveats and Options

1. Choose another "to be avoided" topic in the target culture. After eliciting student feelings or past experiences concerning the topic, have them work in small groups to write a short dialogue such as the one used in class. This can be read or role played to the entire class.
2. If a multicultural class, form students into groups of similar cultural backgrounds and ask them to write a list of "to be avoided" topics for their own culture. Based on one or two of these topics, the groups write a short dialogue between a native speaker in their culture and a second language student studying in their country. The students can act out the dialogues and ask the other students to identify the "to be avoided" topic for the native culture of the actors.

Reference and Further Reading

Johnson, C. (1992). Cultural situations for intercultural understanding. *MEXTESOL Journal, 16*(2/3), 9–20.

Appendix: Sample Dialogue

Linguistic Focus: greetings, clarifying information, exaggeration, differences between formal writing and informal speech, culturally accepted names, perfect tenses, restating information

Pragmatic Focus: choice of topics, what to do when you do not want to continue with the present topic

Brandy: Hi Kim. What 'ya been up to?
Kim: Hi Brandy . . . . (*pause*) . . . . I'm sorry but I didn't understand your question. Could you repeat it please?

Brandy:	Oh, sure. I said "What 'ya been up to?" That means, "What have you been doing recently? Have you been doing anything new?"
Kim:	Now I understand. I don't think I'll ever learn all your expressions in English. No, I've done nothing new or different. Everything is the same: going to school and learning English.
Brandy:	Don't worry, you're doing great in English! I wish I spoke another language nearly as well! Hey, look what I just bought. I saw these red shoes in the store window and just <u>had</u> to have them! I really shouldn't have done it.
Kim:	(*I wonder why she said she "shouldn't have"? She's not married. She has no one to be mad at her for buying them.*) They're beautiful! How much did they cost?
Brandy:	. . . . (pause) . . . . Well, more than I can afford. I probably <u>won't eat for a week now</u> but I really liked them.
Kim:	Were they really <u>that</u> expensive? . . . . (*They don't look so expensive. I wonder why she said that?*) . . . . What was the price? How much did you pay?
Brandy:	No, I'm only exaggerating but, they were expensive. Well, have to go now. See 'ya round. Bye.
Kim:	Bye . . . . (*Why did she leave so quickly and without answering my question?*)

Contributor

Connie R. Johnson teaches in the EFL program as well as the Applied Linguistics Master's Program at the Universidad de las Américas Puebla in Mexico.

Let Me Talk!
(Conversational Overlap)

Level
Advanced

Aims
Become aware of
different styles of and
practice strategies that
will be useful in
conversation with
varying amounts of
overlap

Class Time
1 hour

Preparation Time
10 minutes

Resources
List of controversial
topics

This activity creates a situation in which students can observe their own behavior and the behavior of their classmates in a lively conversation. It provides the basis for a discussion about how these behaviors may vary from person to person, situation to situation, and culture to culture.

Procedure

1. Put students in small groups and tell them to define "interruption in conversation" and "overlap in conversation" and to decide whether the two are different and how. If they need help, ask them to think about what actually happens during an interruption/overlap, how the people involved feel when it happens, and what the speakers' intentions are in the various situations. Students do not need to agree completely because their own experiences will give them different interpretations of interruption and overlap in conversation.

2. Choose a controversial topic (e.g., capital punishment, legalization of drugs, smoking in public places). Any topic will do, but it must be something that holds the students' interest, and it must be something on which the class is divided more or less down the middle.

3. Survey the students on their opinions, and divide the class into two groups, putting those students with similar opinions in the same group. Give each group 5–10 minutes to discuss their side of the issue and prepare for a debate (e.g., make a list of ideas and examples that support their point of view, think about what vocabulary they will need to discuss the issue).

4. Choose one student from each group and sit them face to face at the front of the classroom. Tell these students to discuss the topic, but to

never speak at the same time. No matter how excited they get, the rule is that they must always wait until the other speaker has finished. Tell the other students in the class to listen very carefully and pay attention to the way the two speakers are interacting. After a few minutes, stop the conversation.

5. Choose a different student from each group and sit them face to face at the front of the classroom. Tell these students to discuss the topic, but to speak at the same time as much as possible. They should not wait for the other speaker to finish; as soon as they think of something to say, they should say it. Tell the other students to listen very carefully and pay attention to the way the two speakers are interacting. After a few minutes, stop the conversation.

6. Ask students to sit in a circle and discuss the following questions: What was the difference between the two conversations? How did you (the first two speakers) feel during the first conversation? How did you (the second two speakers) feel during the second conversation? Think about how you act/speak when you are talking to your friends in your native language; are you more like the speakers in the first conversation or the speakers in the second conversation? How do you act/speak when you are speaking to your teacher? boss? family members? Do you think you act this way because of your personality? the personality of the other speakers? the situation? Do other speakers of your language act the same way?

Caveats and Options

1. This activity can serve as the basis for a discussion of the conversational styles of different cultures, or offer practice to students who may find themselves with speakers who have a different style from their own.

2. Think of polite strategies for "interrupting" (e.g., gestures or facial expressions that indicate someone's desire to talk, phrases such as *Excuse me, but . . .* and *May I add something?*). Discuss the places in a speaker's speech where it is appropriate or natural to start overlap.

3. If students are in the country where the target language is spoken, send them out to observe conversations between native speakers in order to confirm their conclusions about overlapping speech during a conversation.

Contributor

Anne Berry is a teacher of EFL and administrator at Atlantic Group-American European Cultural Association in Madrid, Spain. She has studied and written about the different conversational styles of Spanish speakers from Spain and English speakers from the United States.

"Vulgar" Words Through Culture and Context

Levels
Intermediate +

Aims
Acquire the sociolinguistic skill of identifying under which circumstances taboo words are being employed by native speakers of the second language and for what purpose

Class Time
40 minutes

Preparation Time
5 minutes

Resources
Opportunity to observe native speakers of the second language interacting in a natural setting

This activity gives students an opportunity to listen to authentic language with the purpose of identifying any vulgar words or expressions that second language speakers hear being used and to determine if the words are being used appropriately in the situations.

Procedure

1. At the end of a class session, the instructor should initiate a discussion concerning student attitudes toward the use of taboo words and phrases in their first languages. Do they use them? When do they say them? Which do they know in their second language and do they think it important to have them included in a second language class?

2. For homework, have students observe groups of native speakers interacting; students should try to identify words or expressions they consider to be coarse or rude for the situations in which the interactions occurred. They must decide the purpose for which the words were used (e.g., as a joke, before or during a physical or verbal conflict, as an expression of surprise).

3. The following day, divide the group into smaller groups (three to four students) for a discussion about which words/phrases they heard, what the scenarios were at the time, and why the expressions were used.

4. Next, ask the same groups to reflect upon their own languages and cultures. In the situations and for the purposes observed, what would be said in the first language?

5. For the final 15 minutes of the class, have each group report briefly on their findings, including the situation, words, purpose, and how this would be translated into their first language and culture.

6. Intervene when misconceptions on the part of the students arise and are not corrected by other learners. Also, try to have available additional information concerning other situations and purposes for the use of the vulgar words/expressions that are not mentioned by the students.

Caveats and Options

1. This activity can present an opportunity to initiate or enlarge upon the students' sense of registers or levels of language and the recognition of different situations when types of expressions can be used.
2. When, in what situation, and with which interlocutors could a word or expression change from one with the intention of being humorous to one meant to hurt?
3. Engage the group in a discussion of when words that are not vulgar in certain instances can change in other circumstances.
4. Discuss the direct translation into the L2 of socially unacceptable expressions in the learners' L1, specify situations in which they would be used, and talk about how these expression would change in the L2.

Contributor

Connie R. Johnson teaches in the EFL program as well as the Applied Linguistics Master's Program at the Universidad de las Américas Puebla, in Mexico.

What Do You Mean by Polite??!!

Levels
Advanced

Aims
Understand and put into action the U.S. polite fiction that "you and I are equals" and "you and I are relaxed"

Class Time
60-90 minutes

Preparation Time
5 minutes

Resources
Copy of the role play and discussion question handouts for each student

Often, when Asian students visit the United States, they are struck by the directness of North Americans. As students adjust to U.S. life, they too learn to be more direct. Unfortunately, some are unaware that a subtle indirectness also exists within U.S. culture. This activity introduces students to the notion of *polite fictions* and gives them an opportunity to role play situations in which they will be providing positive as well as negative feedback to their subordinate(s).

Procedure

1. First, give a short lecture based on the situation below; or use it as a dictation exercise:

> According to Sakamoto and Naotsuka (1982), "Every culture has its own polite fictions. Whenever we want to be polite, we must act out certain fictions, regardless of the facts. For example, when you meet someone, you may or may not like him, but either way, you must politely pretend to like him" (p. 3). There are many Japanese polite fictions that contrast with the corresponding U.S. polite fictions. Some examples are:
>
> 1. The U.S. polite fiction that "you and I are equals" contrasts with the Japanese polite fiction that "you are my superior." In the United States, the belief that "all men are created equal" lies at the core of social graces. Let us say that you are dining with the president of your company. You might call him Mr. Smith as opposed to Bob, but your actions as well as the language you speak would not differ too much from when you are speaking to a friend. Let us now say that dining with

you and Mr. Smith is a much older man. Although he may make remarks about his age, you should politely not mention it. After all, the polite fiction in the United States is "you and I are equal." Even when asking your subordinate to do something, or when correcting his or her mistakes, you would have to treat him or her as an equal by asking nicely rather than ordering or scolding them.

2. The U.S. polite fiction that "you and I are relaxed" contrasts with the Japanese polite fiction "I'm busy on your behalf." If you are on the way to take a difficult exam, a North American is likely to say "take it easy!" while a Japanese is likely to say "*gambatte*" (work hard!).

If you go to a Japanese home for dinner, the hostess will often be running around cooking or bringing you food and drinks. On the other hand, if you go to a European American home in the United States, the hostess would probably sit with you and pretend that she went to no trouble at all for you. She might have, however, spent the whole day cooking for you.

This same polite fiction can be seen at the workplace. For example, if you ask a Japanese subordinate to do something for you in a hurry, he or she will probably run around looking very busy. On the other hand, if you ask a U.S. subordinate to do something in a hurry, he or she might walk calmly with confidence to his or her desk and work on it as fast as he or she can. Again, the polite fiction "I'm busy on your behalf" contrasts with "you and I are relaxed."

2. Pass out the role-play handouts. Divide students into pairs, and read through Role Play 1.
3. Ask for a volunteer to help you demonstrate how you would approach Role Play 1.
4. Go over the hints. As a general rule, students should remember to always sandwich a negative comment with two positive ones when giving feedback.

5. The pairs should then take turns being Cathy and the Japanese manager.
6. Once the pairs have had sufficient practice, have two pairs combine with each other. One pair performs while the other watches. Then have groups go through the discussion questions. Pairs should then switch roles.
7. Repeat Steps 2–6.

Caveats and Options

1. Role plays can and should be tailored to best suit your students' interests. For example, if your students are mainly education majors, you should use teacher-student interactions. For freshmen and sophomores, student-student interactions might prove to be more practical.

Reference

Sakamoto, N., & Naotsuka, R. (1982). *Polite fictions: Why Japanese and Americans seem rude to each other.* Tokyo: Kinseido.

Appendix: Role Plays and Discussion Questions

Role Play 1

You are a Japanese manager working at a subsidiary in the United States. You are now meeting with your subordinate Cathy.

Your Task: You need to ask Cathy to work on the 3M project and have her complete it by May 3.

Background Information: Cathy does excellent work but often misses deadlines. You need this project completed on time or else your company may lose this contract.

Hints:
- First, thank her for coming.
- Ask her to sit down.
- Make sure you praise Cathy for her good work.
- Tell her how important this project is and that she was chosen because of her superior work.
- Explain to her that if you do not meet the deadline, you may lose your client entirely.

- Ask her if you can do anything to help her meet the deadline.
- If you can, use jokes to soften the mood, especially when you are giving constructive criticism.
- Don't forget that in the United States, "you and I are equals" and "you and I are relaxed" are two prevalent polite fictions.

Role Play 2

You are a Japanese manager working at a subsidiary in the United States. You are now meeting with your subordinate John. John has been late to work for the past 2 weeks.

Your Task: You need to find out what is wrong and make sure that John is no longer late.

Background Information: John has worked for your company for the past 10 years. He has been a hard worker and has rarely been late. You, therefore, have reason to believe that he might have some personal problems causing his tardiness. Although you would like to help him with his problems, you want to make sure you are not invading his privacy.

Hints:
- First, thank John for coming.
- Ask him how he's doing.
- Tell him that you know that he has worked for the company for the past 10 years and has been doing an outstanding job.
- Tell him that you have noticed that he has been late for the past 2 weeks and you are concerned about it.
- Ask him if there is anything going on that you should know about.
- Ask him if you can help with anything.
- If you can, use jokes to soften the mood, especially when you are giving constructive criticism.
- Don't forget that in the United States, "you and I are equals" and "you and I are relaxed" are two prevalent polite fictions.

Discussion Questions

When giving feedback, make sure that you give positive comments when you give negative ones.

Partner:

- How did it feel?
- Did you feel that your boss respected you?

Observers:

- Did the person come across as treating the subordinate fairly?
- Would you like to work under him or her?
- How were his or her nonverbals? Did he or she look the subordinate in the eye?
- Did he or she seem relaxed and confident or did he or she look tense and unsure?

Contributor

Tomoko Yoshida Isogai is a lecturer at Keio University. He also conducts cross-cultural training workshops for private as well as public organizations in Japan.

Part IV: Activities for Culture Exploration

Essa Al-Abbas and Satoko Tamiya at Northern Virginia Community College, Alexandria, Virginia USA.

Ethnographic Study: Dynamic Seeing for Culture Learning

Levels
Any

Aims
Learn another culture
Become aware of the
complexity of learning
culture

Class Time
30 minutes

Preparation Time
Variable

Resources
Churches, bars, health
clubs, courthouses, or
any other meeting
places where people
gather for a specific
purpose

This activity focuses on what happens as individuals observe, learn, and adapt to a new culture. It helps students examine their own processes of culture learning and become more skilled at coming to understand unfamiliar and familiar cultures.

Procedure

1. Prepare the class by discussing with students how they use their powers of observation—seeing, hearing, smelling, feeling—to learn about a new place.
2. Ask students to close their eyes and describe as many details about the classroom as they can. They should include details that are visual, auditory, and olfactory, as well as anything they might have noticed.
3. Talk about the value of using all one's senses to understand a new culture.
4. Have students choose groups to work with or place them in groups of two or three people. Each group should then choose a site (from a list of sites provided) that they will visit and observe.
5. Either during class time—or as a homework assignment—have students visit the sites and observe for at least 30 minutes, taking notes either during or after the observation. Tell them not to discuss their sites or their observations with other group members until they return to class.
6. In class, lead the groups in a discussion of what they observed using the following procedure as an example:
    *   Have students read their observation notes to other members of their group.

- Ask students to note similarities and differences in what they observed.
- Ask students to comment on how their observations reflect who they are (e.g., their own culture, previous experiences, likes and dislikes).
- Ask students to share what they are learning about their site, their culture, and themselves.
- Have students talk about what they are going to focus on or try to learn in their next observation (at the same site).

7. Have students continue observations and process them using the questions above and begin to look at issues of participation, membership, and belonging in that site.

8. Ask students to make hypotheses about the culture of the site they are learning.

9. Ask students to identify an individual to interview at their site to act as an informant who will help them confirm or disprove their hypotheses about the site.

10. Encourage in-class discussions of both the observations and interviews to help students begin to look at culture from different perspectives, to realize the interplay between emic and etic perspectives, and to begin to develop empathy for different perspectives.

Caveats and Options

1. To use the activity in teacher training, it is important to employ various frameworks for culture learning (e.g., Bennett, 1993; Damen, 1987; Fantini, 1984; Moran, n.d.) to help link their experience to a theoretical perspective.

2. Depending on the interest and readiness of students and teacher, this activity can work at varying levels of self-disclosure and depth.

3. Ask students to bring back identity kits (Gee, 1990) and/or artifacts (Gaston, 1984) from their sites and discuss how they reflect both the culture of the site and their own view of culture.

4. Ask students to concentrate on their culture learning strategies, compare them with those of other students, and apply these strategies in other situations.

5. The teacher's participation in this activity along with students models culture learning and demonstrates that everyone is a culture learner—even of one's own culture.
6. This process for learning culture is slow. It is useful to acknowledge this with students and discuss how learning culture, in general, is a slow process.

References and Further Reading

Bennett, M. (1993). Towards ethnorelativism: A developmental model of intercultural sensitivity. In R. M. Paige (Ed.), *Education for the intercultural experience* (pp. 21–71). Yarmouth, ME: Intercultural Press.

Damen, L. (1987). *Culture learning: The fifth dimension in the language classroom*. Reading, MA: Addison-Wesley.

Fantini, A. E. et al. (1984). *Cross-cultural orientation: A guide for leaders and educators*. Brattleboro, VT: The Experiment Press.

Gaston, J. (1984). *Cultural awareness teaching techniques*. Brattleboro, VT: Pro Lingua Associates.

Gee, J. (1990). *Social linguistics and literacies: Ideology in discourses*. London: Falmer Press.

Moran, P. (n.d.). *A framework for culture teaching*. Unpublished manuscript.

Contributors

Marti Anderson, Michael Jerald, and Leslie Turpin are faculty in the Master of Arts in Teaching Program at the School for International Training in Brattleboro, Vermont, in the United States.

What's Going On Here?
(Culture Contexts)

Levels
Any

Aims
Experience an event in
the target culture
Figure out what's going
on contextually with
and without the use of
language

Class Time
20–30 minutes

Preparation Time
5 minutes

Resources
5-minute segment of an
appropriate movie
recorded on videotape

This activity utilizes the power of video to bring a cultural segment to the classroom experience, allowing students to test their understanding with and without language by tuning in to contextual information and trying to make sense of what they see. A favorite segment, for example, may be taken from *The Bill Cosby Show* or a similar sitcom.

Procedure

1. Select a 5-minute segment of a movie. Try to choose one that depicts a brief incident that is comprehensible even without knowing the entire film sequence.

2. Play the segment first without the sound track (volume turned off) and ask students to figure out: who the people involved are; how they are related to each other; where they are; what they are doing; what they are saying; and what the story line is.

3. When the segment is over, ask the students to discuss their answers to the questions, attempting to create the story line together.

4. Ask what clues (e.g., nonverbal, contextual) helped them figure the story out.

5. Play the segment again, this time with the sound track (volume turned on), and ask the students to reconsider their original interpretation.

6. Discuss any revisions they may have made in the story and what these were based on (e.g., was it the way something was said affectively, or did they understand some of the words or expressions that influenced the revision?).

Caveats and Options

1. This activity can be used with students at all levels of language proficiency. Beginners with little or no verbal comprehension can rely on contextual cues and affective aspects of language, and advanced students can try to match their initial inferences with what they understood when the volume was turned up.

2. Intermediate- to advanced-level students can also be asked to explore cultural and contextual aspects in greater depth because they will understand more of the spoken dialogue.

3. This activity can be followed with intercultural exploration by discussing what misinterpretations were made and why, and how our native language and culture influence how we make sense of any given situation (i.e., how our "cultural lens" works).

References and Further Reading

Fantini, A. E. et al. (1984). *Cross-cultural orientation: A guide for leaders and educators.* Brattleboro, VT: The Experiment Press.

Contributor

Alvino E. Fantini, senior faculty member at the School for International Training, Brattleboro, Vermont, in the United States, is a past president of SIETAR International (Society for Intercultural Education, Training, and Research) and an international consultant on matters of language and intercultural communications.

Everyday Tasks (Operations)

Levels
Any

Aims
Experience an everyday
task common to the
target culture
Develop vocabulary and
other expressions
appropriate to the task
Practice language in
context

Class Time
20–30 minutes

Preparation Time
5 minutes

Resources
Jar of peanut butter, jar
of grape jelly, loaf of
white bread, dish, knife,
napkin, table

This activity falls into a category of tasks sometimes known as *operations*, that is, ordinary activities found in everyday life that often contain specific cultural information. The activity offers an amusing yet real way of experiencing an aspect of a common experience of many young U.S. school children by preparing a peanut butter and jelly sandwich in the classroom while learning relevant vocabulary and practicing language. This activity and others like it have been used over many years by teachers at our institution. The originator is unknown.

Procedure

1. After placing students in a semicircle so all can see, prepare a peanut butter and jelly sandwich in front of the class.
2. Before beginning the task, describe some of its cultural context (e.g., many U.S. schoolchildren like to take these sandwiches for lunch or for a snack; they often enjoy this with milk).
3. While preparing the sandwich, describe its preparation step by step (e.g., first you take two slices of soft white bread, choose the preferred type of peanut butter, spread the grape jelly over the peanut butter, cut off the crust, and then cut the sandwich into small triangles).
4. After talking through the steps while making the sandwich, ask students to do a variety of things, for example: restate the steps (in the present tense), restate the procedure (in the past tense), direct you or another student to do the activity once again (using the imperative).
5. Have students discuss their reactions to this cultural event and why (offer sandwich wedges to those who wish to taste this snack); then have them comment on favorite snacks in their culture(s) (e.g., who

prepares them, who eats them and who does not, whether the snack is a personal favorite or common in the culture).

6. Repeat the operation, having students provide instructions. Follow these literally and precisely and often funny things will result, pointing to the need for linguistic accuracy and precision. You may then repeat a third time, having students direct another student and interrupting periodically to ask: What did he or she just do? or what is he or she going to do next? In this way you can elicit other forms of the verb in the past or future.

Caveats and Options

1. This activity can emphasize language use, culture exploration, or both, depending on the course needs. It can also lead to intercultural exploration by stressing comparative and contrastive aspects of common tasks.

2. Think of other operations or everyday tasks performed in the target culture around which you can develop further lessons.

3. Have students think of everyday tasks common to their own native culture and come to class prepared to demonstrate and explain to other students.

Contributor

Alvino E. Fantini, senior faculty member at the School for International Training, Brattleboro, Vermont, in the United States, is a past president of SIETAR International (Society for Intercultural Education, Training, and Research) and an international consultant on matters of language and intercultural communications.

Families in Situation Comedies

Levels
Low intermediate +

Aims
Achieve a deeper
understanding of family
roles in U.S. culture
Develop the appropriate
vocabulary to discuss
cultural issues related to
the family
Practice listening skills
such as predicting and
inferencing
Appreciate the changing
nature of culture

Class Time
5-6 hours over
4-6 weeks

Preparation Time
45-60 minutes for the
first video; 35-40
minutes for each
successive video

Resources
TV, VCR, videocassettes,
syndicated U.S. televison
situation comedies
(sitcoms)

Spanning more than 40 years, U.S. sitcoms provide a rich, easily accessible resource for cultural investigations by teachers and students, especially in EFL situations. Using sitcoms in the classroom has a variety of benefits—from developing students' language skills (listening and speaking) to sharpening their observation and inferencing skills.

Procedure

1. While previewing a sitcom from the 1950s, write down the plot and the main characters. Write one or two basic comprehension questions for each part of the episode. (Sitcoms follow the basic pattern of (a) emergence of problem; (b) characters dealing with the problem; and (c) resolution.) You may also note any essential vocabulary or idioms.

2. In class, lead a discussion on roles in the family (male/female and parents/children), having students first focus on families in their countries (see Appendix for some suggestions).

3. Ask the students to imagine that their parents are answering the same questions but 20-25 years ago. Would the answers be the same? Why? Why not?

4. Ask students to apply the same discussion questions to current U.S. families; tell them they can base their answers on observations they have made from the media or real experiences with U.S. families.

5. Tell the students that to gain a better understanding of the present day U.S. family, they will be watching a selection of TV programs from the last 40 years.

6. Elicit information about sitcoms from the students, including whether they watch them, why, which ones they like, what the programs have in common. Write their responses on the board. Be sure that the following information is covered:
   - Sitcoms follow a basic pattern (see Step 1 above).
   - They have a set cast of main characters.
   - They are 30 minutes long (22 minutes without commercials).
7. Tell the students that the first video they are going to watch is from the 1950s. (*Father Knows Best* works well for the first selection.) Ask them what they know about the era and write information on the board.
8. Write the name of the show on the board, and when appropriate (as in *Father Knows Best*), ask the students to discuss the title and make predictions.
9. Write the names of the characters on the board and who they are (e.g., Jim Anderson, father), and have the students write the same information in their notebooks.
10. Show the students the first part of the video—when the problem emerges—and ask them two or three comprehension questions. Give students time to write additional information next to the characters' names as they learn more about them. Replay Part 1 if students request it.
11. Repeat this step for Parts 2 and 3 of the video.
12. Once the students have finished watching the video, ask them if anything surprised them (e.g., language, fashion, interpersonal relationships).
13. Ask the students to apply the questions that they answered about families in their own countries to the family in the sitcom.
14. Encourage students to be as detailed as possible in their answers, and to support their answers with examples.
15. In approximately 1 week, show a second sitcom from the next era. That is, if you started with a program from the 1950s, the next program would be from the 1960s.

16. Repeat Steps 7–15 until you have shown a sitcom from the 1990s.

17. Throughout the process, constantly encourage students to answer why and how any changes in roles occurred. For example, ask them what kinds of events were happening in the society that might have triggered changes.

18. Throughout the process, have students look for similarities between U.S. families from different eras and families in their own countries. For example, which era in the sitcoms comes closest to the current situation in their countries? As in Step 17, encourage students to try to answer how different events in their countries have influenced family roles.

Caveats and Options

1. It is important to remember that sitcoms are one resource when exploring a variety of sociocultural issues, but they are not the definitive source. Students should be asked to explore the role of media in shaping and informing culture: Are TV programs trying to mirror reality or project an ideal? Who do they try to include and who do they exclude?

2. Once students are familiar with the basic elements of sitcoms, they can choose other topics to explore on their own, such as the mainstream society's view of minorities, women in the workplace, or dating. Students can present their observations to the class.

3. Using sitcoms can be tailored to high beginning- or low intermediate-level students by viewing the programs without the sound. By focusing on the settings, lower level students can still gain valuable cultural information.

4. Students could survey native speakers, asking them which shows were popular when they were growing up and how they felt about them.

5. You can tailor the viewing procedure to fit the needs of your students. For example, decide which kind of previewing and schema-building activities would be best for your class.

**Appendix:
Resource
Material**

The titles of some family sitcoms that work well in classes appear below, followed by sample discussion questions.

From the 1950s: *Father Knows Best, Ozzie and Harriet, Leave it to Beaver*
From the 1960s: *The Dick Van Dyke Show, Bewitched*
From the 1970s: *The Brady Bunch, The Partridge Family, One Day at a Time, The Jeffersons, What's Happening?*
From the 1980s: *The Cosby Show, Growing Pains, Family Ties*
From the 1990s: *Roseanne, Full House, Blossom*

Questions for Discussion of Family Roles

1. What are the responsibilities of the father/mother/children in your country? (If this question is too broad for the students, you may pose the following more specific questions.)
2. Who earns more money?
3. Who manages the money?
4. Who disciplines the children? How are children disciplined?
5. If there is a family conflict, who decides what will happen?
6. What are three things that the father does around the house?
7. What are three things that the mother does around the house?
8. What are three things that the children do around the house?
9. Can you imagine the mother doing some of the father's work? If so, what? If not, why not? What about the reverse?
10. Describe the relationship between husband and wife, father and children, mother and children, brother and sister.

Contributor

Judy Sharkey is an EFL instructor at Kansai Gaidai College in Hirakata City, Japan.

Home Sweet Home

Levels
Intermediate +

Aims
Use language and critical thinking skills to describe homes and regions of the world by categorizing and summarizing information related to the environment and the social structure

Class Time
6–12 hours/unit

Preparation Time
1–2 hours

Resources
Pictures of homes (a minimum of three) seen from the outside and including some surrounding landscape
Travel magazines (e.g., *National Geographic* or *Houses and Homes*)
Overhead projector (OHP), transparencies, and markers

Procedure

1. Ask students to examine pictures of different homes and then to choose the home that interests each of them the most. Have them tell two partners why they like that house or why they find it interesting.

2. Ask students to then do a quick-write (maximum 15 minutes), choosing one of the following options:

   - Describe the family that lives in that home. You may wish to include what the parents do for a living, how many children there are and what they like to do for fun, and what the family likes to do together (use your imagination).

   - Write about relationships. Would you predict that people have strong, interdependent relationships? What would you predict would be most important to people living in that house: status, fame, money, or friendship? Why?

   - Would you feel comfortable living in that house? Why or why not? What would be the best thing about living in that place? The worst?

3. Ask the students to look carefully at a home selected by the teacher. Consider the house's relationship to the Earth. What can you guess about the environment around that house? Consider:

   - climate
   - geography
   - seasons
   - flora and fauna
   - people's livelihoods
   - energy use

4. Verbally brainstorm as a group about climate and seasons (write ideas on chalkboard). Note and provide useful vocabulary if needed with semantic organizers (e.g., word map or feature grid, as in Vacca & Vacca, 1993, chapter 4).

5. Assign a different category (i.e., see those listed in Step 3) to each small group of students. Students should make predictions as to where the home is located, listing as many ideas as possible related to their category. Each group shares their ideas as the group constructs an environmental profile of the region.

6. The class then decides together where they think the home is located, to be followed by a discussion of other things they know about that region. The teacher should guide the discussion to a brainstorming session regarding what they think the social framework is like in that region. The class together builds a societal profile, considering:

   ● family structure (e.g., do grandparents live nearby?)
   ● parental authority
   ● religious and leisure pursuits
   ● male/female roles
   ● emphasis on rules, obedience, conformity
   ● degree of emphasis on modernization, conveniences

7. Ask students to now work in small groups to choose a picture of a home they are all interested in and to make environmental and societal profiles as in the previous activities. Tell the group that they will be working together to construct a transparency outline for a group report.

8. Model how to give a short (maximum 10-minute) report, using the picture of the home in Steps 3-6 and the class outline on transparency. Decide upon a presentation schedule so that each group can prepare their transparency and practice outside of class. Insist that each group member participate in giving the verbal report and describe how it will be graded (consider grading both the outline and the presentation). Assist with extra library work if they wish to expand their knowledge.

9. Conduct group presentations, score, and debrief.

10. Ask each person to prepare his or her own environmental and societal profile on transparency, describing his or her own home and region. Help each person find additional reference materials.

11. Once each person has had time to gather information about his or her region, ask each to verbally report the most interesting information back to a "help" group. The group should ask questions to clarify and should make suggestions for organizing the information and making the presentation more interesting.

12. Each class member then presents a short (5- to 7-minute) presentation about his or her region, using the outline for reference and commenting on both the environmental and the social framework.

13. If possible, work with local schools to see if students can present their regional summaries to schoolchildren in various classrooms.

Caveats and Options

1. You may wish to focus on regions of the United States and to supplement with video- or audio-based materials depicting regional differences.

2. The teacher should also complete the writing assignment in Step 2, then orchestrate sharing of papers as each writer finishes. Encourage students to read as many responses as possible. You may also wish to collect the quick-writes for further editing or revision.

3. If you do not have time for an entire unit on this topic, Steps 1 and 4–6 should be conducted, with others optional.

4. Both the outline and oral summary could be scored, with points assigned to the following categories: content, organization, language use, and comprehensibility; with feedback provided as to fluency, style and problem utterances. It is also a good idea to time the reports and to deduct points if the presenter(s) go under or over time. (This encourages rehearsal.)

References and Further Reading

Laird, E. (1993). *Faces of the USA.* New York: Longman.

Morris, A. (1992). *Houses and homes.* New York: Lothrop, Lee, & Shepard Books.

Turner Educational Services, Inc. (1992). *Across America with Larry Woods* [video]. Atlanta, GA: Turner Multimedia.

Vacca, R. T., & Vacca, J. L. (1993). *Content area reading* (4th ed.). New York: HarperCollins.

World Communications. (1992). *Mini-world videos.* Everett, WA: Author.

Contributor

Kim Hughes Wilhelm is curriculum coordinator for the Center for English as a Second Language, and assistant professor of Linguistics, at Southern Illinois University in Carbondale, Illinois, in the United States.

Guess Who's Coming to Visit?

Levels
Intermediate +

Aims
Discuss racial and cultural tensions observed in the United States
Understand U.S. attitudes about racial and cultural differences, particularly in the context of marriage

Class Time
1 hour

Preparation Time
2 hours

Resources
VCR with television monitor
Videotaped copy of the movie *Guess Who's Coming to Dinner?*
Videotaped copy of the movie *The Joy Luck Club*

Watching brief, well-acted movie excerpts that highlight family reactions to intercultural and interracial couples introduces ESOL students to U.S. attitudes—old and new—about this subject. Additionally, there may be wide variations within the same ESOL class as to what is accepted in the students' home countries. The relationships of couples featured in the movies may be considered unremarkable or completely forbidden.

Procedure

1. Before class, obtain copies of the movies, and fast-forward to the following points:
   - *Joy Luck Club*—the scene in which Waverly brings home her American fiancé to meet and have dinner with her parents
   - *Guess Who's Coming to Dinner?*—the scene in which Joey sits down alone with her mother (Katherine Hepburn) to try to break the news of her African American fiancé (before Sidney Poitier enters the room)
2. In class, introduce the topic in the way you think best suits your class.
3. Play the excerpt from *The Joy Luck Club*.
4. Complete clozed dialogue (see Appendix A) and discuss.
5. Play the *Guess Who's Coming to Dinner?* clip. Beforehand, ask students to note reactions of the following three people: the mother, the housekeeper, the father. Stop the tape after the father (Spencer Tracy) has heard and understood the news that the couple intends to marry.
6. Hold a class discussion.
7. Assign homework (Appendix B), or do written exercise in class.

Caveats and Options

1. Writing assignment: What would your parents do if you brought home a fiancé(é) of another race or culture? (This question helps to elicit hypothetical conditional sentences).
2. Writing assignment: An argumentation essay with the title "Why Successful Intercultural Marriage Is (or Is Not) Possible."
3. Class discussion with personal relevance: Talk about cultural and racial difficulties and conflicts students may have observed while in the United States, or in their own countries.
4. Explain the recent history of the U.S. civil rights movement. Compare the 1960s with the 1990s.
5. Advanced classes may enjoy reading chapters from Romano's (1988) *Intercultural Marriage.*

References and Further Reading

Romano, D. (1988). *Intercultural marriage.* Yarmouth, ME: Intercultural Press.

Appendix

Handout 1: Cloze Exercise

Directions: The following is a partial dialogue from the film, The Joy Luck Club. *During this portion of the film, Waverly, a Chinese American woman, brings her red-haired, freckled-faced American* fiancé *home to meet her parents. After watching the film, complete this exercise with appropriate words. (They need not always be the same as the film.)*

The next week, I brought Rich _____ Mom's birthday dinner. Sort of a "surprise present." I figured she was going to have to _____ Rich, like it or not.

"Rich, _____ is my father."

"Happy Birthday, Ma . . . and Ma, this is Rich."

"Boy, something smells wonderful. I guess we came to the right place, huh? You know, Waverly has been _____ me that you are the best cook."

"I think maybe we go her . . . ."

"So many spots _____ his face."

Of course, the night was still young. Thank God I'd already _____ him _____ the "Emily Post" of Chinese manners. Actually, _____ were a few things I forgot to mention . . . . He shouldn't have _____ that second glass when everyone else had had only half an inch "just for taste."

"Shrimp! _____ favorite!"

He should have taken only a small spoonful of the best dish until everyone had had a _____."

"He has good appetite."

He shouldn't have bragged _____ was a _____ learner. But the worst was _____ Rich criticized my mother's cooking, and he didn't _____ what he had done. As is _____ Chinese cooks' custom, my mother always _____ her own cooking, but only with the dishes she serves _____ special pride.

"This dish not salty enough—no flavor. Is too bad _____ eat. But please . . . ."

That was our cue to eat _____, and proclaim it the best she'd ever made.

"You know, Linda . . . all this needs is a _____ soy sauce."

(Later, in the car)

"So, how _____ your Mom react when you told her _____ the wedding?"

"She'd rather get rectal cancer."

"How come?"

Handout 2: Participles Used As Adjectives

Participles that are used as adjectives can be confusing to nonnative speakers. It sometimes helps to think of relationships such as cause/effect or active/passive when deciding which one to use.

It is shocking to him. *(active, or cause)*
He is shocked by it. *(passive, or effect)*

Or you can learn them naturally, as native speakers do, noticing their use in reading and in conversation. Circle the adjective in the following sentence that best fits the relationship expressed.

The movie *Guess Who's Coming to Dinner?* examines the subject of (mixing/mixed) marriage. The 1967 film tells the story of Joanna Drayton, a white girl, and John Prentice, a (distinguishing/distinguished) black doctor.

While in Hawaii, they meet and make the (surprising/surprised) discovery that they love each other, and they decide to get married. After a long (tiring/tired) flight home, they visit Joanna's parents' home to make their (astonishing/astonished) announcement.

The part of Christina Drayton (Joanna's mother) is played by Katherine Hepburn, a famous American actress. She won the 1967 Academy Award for Best Actress, an accolade she received because of her (convincing/convinced) performance as a (shocking/shocked) and (bewildering/bewildered) mother. Later in the story, she comes to accept her daughter's engagement and feels (pleasing/pleased) about her happiness.

Surprisingly, the Drayton's black housekeeper is very (disturbing/disturbed) by the announcement. She finds the situation (shocking/shocked) and inappropriate. John Prentice remains calm, but he is slightly (embarrassing/embarrassed) by the awkward situation.

Joanna's father, Matthew Drayton, is at first (confusing/confused), and then (upsetting/upset) by the news. He feels the marriage will be a serious problem, and Joanna is (disappointing/disappointed) when her father does not congratulate them immediately.

The movie came out in 1967, during the U.S. civil rights era. It was a controversial, (interesting/interested) film.

Contributor

Jane Conzett teaches ESL at Xavier University in Cincinnati, Ohio, in the United States.

Let's Shop

Level
High beginning–
intermediate

Aim
Use everyday culture as
a means of teaching ESL
reading

Class Time
30–50 minutes

Preparation Time
30 minutes

Resources
Clothing ads, catalogues,
and visuals (e.g., *Oxford
Picture Dictionary*)

With its emphasis on speaking, listening, reading, and writing, the communicative-proficiency approach is conducive to the inclusion of cross-cultural learning experiences. Classroom activities and drills can be designed to integrate structure and sociolinguistic material as well. This exercise shows how culture can be easily integrated into lessons in a way that is interesting and constructive for the learners. A creative teacher can use these activities as a guide in creating additional opportunities for cross-cultural learning

Procedure

1. Introduce concepts related to U.S. (or British, Canadian . . .) shopping customs. Prepare sale ads and catalogues to use as classroom prompts.
2. Students skim the material and scan it for specific information, for example, men's and women's clothing, automotive parts, electronics, looking for prices, sizes, and quality.
3. Prepare a worksheet and have students take turns explaining the listed concepts so everyone, even new arrivals, will have a good shopping experience.
4. Terms and cultural materials relative to other countries can now be introduced and contrasted with L1 concepts.

Caveats and Options

1. Be sure that the class concentrates on the task at hand: reading for cultural information.
2. A possible option would be for students to look for contrasts by focusing on one particular item, for example:
   ● How much is a sweater in this city?
   ● What's expensive for a sweater?

- What's cheap?
- What size do you wear? (Convert your size to centimeters.)
- Which store has the best deal on sweaters?

References and Further Reading

Brown, H. D. (1994). *Principles of language learning and teaching.* Englewood Cliffs, NJ: Prentice Hall.

Carver, T. K., & Fotinos, S. D. (1977). *A conversation book: English in everyday life. Book 2.* Englewood Cliffs, NJ: Prentice Hall.

Omaggio, A. C. (1986). *Teaching language in context.* Boston: Heinle & Heinle.

Appendix: Sample Worksheet

Let's Shop: Vocabulary and Concepts

1. one-day sale
2. semiannual sale
3. catalogue order
4. red tag sale
5. manufacturer's closeout sale
6. chain store
7. good (bad) buy
8. coupons
9. outlet store
10. warehouse clearance

Questions

1. In Mexico, Italy, . . . , who does the shopping?
2. How often do stores have sales?
3. Do people in your country prefer a large department store or smaller specialty shops?
4. Does one pay a fixed price or bargain?
5. What is the most common way of paying?
6. Are these customs changing?

Contributor

Douglas Magrath currently teaches ESL at Seminole Community College, Florida, in the United States. He also taught in Tennessee, and at the American University of Beirut in Lebanon. He has presented at ACTFL and TESOL, and has published in various professional journals.

In the News

Levels
Intermediate +

Aims
Improve vocabulary
Increase and monitor
reading
Develop writing skills
Become aware of
important issues of the
host culture

Class Time
30–90 minutes

Preparation Time
5 minutes–1 hour

Resources
Newspapers and current
event magazines of the
host country

Students' interest in learning is heightened when they feel it has special relevance to them and their future situation. This activity grabs their attention by dealing with the current issues of the culture into which they will soon be entering and by giving them a vocabulary in the host culture language with which to discuss these topics.

Procedure

1. Distribute the article(s) on the topic to be studied or distribute newspapers and magazines if students are to choose an article at large.
2. Allow 10–20 minutes reading time depending on the length of article and level of students.
3. On the chalkboard or a flip chart have students write any words that are new or unfamiliar to them.
4. After everyone has finished reading and listed their words, go through the list with the class. First see if any of the students can define them, then correct or add to the definitions as needed. This provides a good forum for comparing the topics in the students' culture to those of the culture they will be soon entering.
5. After finishing explanations, have students copy all the words.
6. Students should then choose 10 of the words and use them in sentences to demonstrate their understanding of the words. (This can be done orally or in writing; if written it may be done in class or given as homework.)
7. At the end of each week or during the final week of class, test students on their memory of the words (in part or all).

Caveats and Options

1. In addition to or instead of having the students use the words in sentences, the teacher can have the students demonstrate their understanding of the word or words by roleplaying or acting them out.

References and Further Reading

Miller, J. N., & Clark, R. C. (Eds.). (1993). *The world: The 1990's from the pages of a real small-town daily newspaper*. Brattleboro, VT: Pro Lingua Associates.

Contributor

Peter W. Hayward is currently a cultural orientation and language trainer for advanced and intermediate students participating in the International Organization for Migration COLT program in Kenya for refugees resettling to the United States.

Exploring Cultural Values

Level
Intermediate

Aims
Identify mainstream U.S.
cultural values
Relate these values to
specific behaviors

Class Time
Two 30-minute periods

Preparation Time
20 minutes

Resources
Overhead projector
(OHP) and transparency

This activity gives ESL students in the United States a chance to state some of their difficult or inexplicable experiences in dealing with Americans, and provides them with some information that can help them to gain a better understanding of U.S. culture. This activity is designed for the multicultural classroom.

Procedure

1. In one class, have students write a short paragraph (about five or six sentences) on some custom or behavior they have observed in the United States that surprised or confused them. After about 20–30 minutes, collect their papers.
2. After class, read over the students' paragraphs and summarize each student's main issue (e.g., a story about how Americans smile at the student and speak to him, even when they are unacquainted, could be summarized as "Americans smile at and speak to strangers"). List these summarized statements in your notes.
3. Also before the next class meeting, prepare a transparency listing some mainstream U.S. values, for example: control over environment and time, the healthiness of change, equality, individualism, privacy, self-help, future orientation, action orientation, informality, directness, materialism (cf. Levine & Adelman, 1993).
4. In the next class, put the transparency of values on an OHP and discuss these values with the students. Be sure that they understand the concepts by asking for some examples of each value. Ask them if they think these values are held by the Americans they know. Ask them to think of the opposite of each of the values given (see Levine & Adelman, 1993, for contrasting values). Have individual students tell

which values are true of their home cultures. (Be careful not to allow the discussion to drift into an evaluation of the right or wrong of the values. The point here is to just notice the differences, not evaluate or judge.)

5. Write the list of summary statements you made of their paragraphs on the board so that they and the transparency are both visible. (Do not say who wrote which ideas.) Have the students discuss and decide which of the U.S. value(s) are reflected in each summary. For example, a summary that reads "Americans carry calendars and schedule activities carefully" would be an example of the U.S. value of control over time.

Caveats and Options

1. This activity can be expanded into a discussion of how recognizing the U.S. values reflected in certain behaviors can help students understand U.S. culture better.
2. For more advanced students, the teacher can type out (without names, of course) all the paragraphs and give them to the students at the beginning of the second class. In small groups, they can provide the summaries for each paragraph before proceeding with the rest of the activity.

References and Further Reading

Levine, D., & Adelman, M. (1993). *Beyond language: Cross-cultural communication*. Englewood Cliffs, NJ: Prentice Hall.

Contributor

Amy T. Seifer currently teaches intermediate reading in the English for academic purposes program at Georgia State University, Atlanta, in the United States, where she is completing her master's degree in TESL. She previously taught EFL in China for 2 years and is planning to return there after graduation.

Exploring Culture Through Conversational Expressions

Levels
High intermediate +

Aims
Work together to
discover the cultural
implications of language
in everyday
conversation

Class Time
30 minutes–1 hour

Preparation Time
20 minutes

Resources
List of conversational
expressions
Index cards

It is important that students be able to understand the cultural and linguistic implications of English used in conversation. The activities presented require that students assess informal spoken language for its direct and implied meaning. Students need practice in assessing language in this way to assist them in developing an intuitive sense of English.

Procedure

1. Solicit examples of some conversational expressions students have heard on television used by native speakers, or from other second language learners. (The phrase *conversational expressions* refers to commonly used phrases reflecting an informal speaking style that is idiomatic and dialectal in nature.) You might offer such commonly heard examples as:
   - *to give one a ring* (to telephone someone)
   - *to keep a stiff upper lip* (to be strong)
   - *to get burned* (to be deceived by someone)
   - *to lighten up* (to become relaxed about something)
   - *What's up?* (How are you? What's new?)
   - *Catch you later.* (Bye. See you later.)
   - *Quit pulling my leg.* (Stop kidding around.)
   - *That's really off the wall.* (That's very odd.)
2. Write the idioms on the board and discuss what they mean, their cultural significance, the identity of the speakers within the social context, and how the expressions are used.
3. Have students work in small groups to brainstorm at least four more such expressions. Ask students to discuss their understanding of the expressions according to the criteria listed in Step 2. Have the group

write sentences illustrating how their expressions might be used. Students need to be prepared to share their findings with the whole class.

4. In the meantime, circulate to give groups any needed support to interpret the expressions.

5. Have groups join those from other groups to discuss and share their findings. Each small group should then make changes to their sentences based on class feedback to their contributions.

6. Ask each group to prepare a final version of the set of conversational expressions on index cards. Information on the card needs to include: the meaning, the cultural significance, speaker identity within the social context, and how each saying is used. Students should then circulate the cards among themselves.

Caveats and Options

1. To guide students when preparing cards, it would be helpful to explain and have a large model written out on a flip chart to illustrate the information each card needs to include.

2. Show students a videotape of a situation comedy.

3. Ask students to listen for, and take notes on, at least four conversational expressions that are new to them from the program. Students should be prepared to share their findings with the whole class.

4. Divide students into pairs to brainstorm a list of corresponding conversational expressions from their own culture(s). These are to be added to the list compiled from the situation comedy.

Contributor

Virginia M. Tong is assistant professor at Hunter College of the City University of New York, in the United States, where she teaches methodology of TESOL and general linguistics. Her research interests are acculturation and sociolinguistics.

Room Walk

Levels
Intermediate +

Aims
Understand the cultural significance of some objects or physical features in an everyday setting as seen through the eyes of a participant
Try to satisfy curiosity about another culture
Practice using spatial prepositions and descriptions

Class Time
1 hour

Preparation Time
5 minutes

Resources
Picture of a culture-oriented object/feature in a room

The cultural implications of a physical object/feature in one culture can be described by a participant of that culture in a fascinating manner.

Procedure

1. Explain how a room in a culture can have a special feature or object unique to that culture, around which many activities and memories of the occupants are centered, for example, a place of worship in a Japanese home, the heated floor in a Korean home, an open fireplace in a Western house, or a Buddhist statue at a certain temple.
2. Introduce and demonstrate spatial prepositions and explain how to describe a room according to spatial order, centering on a culture-related dominant aspect. At the same time, illustrate this aloud with a personal example.
3. Practice questions that can help students pursue and satisfy their sense of curiosity about another culture, for example, questions related to size, appearance in more detail, family/social activities and traditions in relation to the object, different attitudes toward the object depending on age/sex/status, how it was made, its value, and so on.
4. Have students draw a special room in their own house, or one from their memory of a school, temple, or relative's room that has a culture-related dominant aspect.
5. Ask the students, without showing the picture, to describe that room to a partner or a group of students. The listener(s) must draw a picture of the room and objects being described (the main purpose here being to allow the listener(s) to step into the room and sense the atmosphere of the room and some major objects in it while listening to the description).

6. After students have compared pictures to make sure that they are the same and no major points are missing, they can pursue discussion about meanings and culture-related aspects/memories and personal experiences of significance (including those questions previously practiced). After all, even people of the same culture will have their own particular episodes associated with these common cultural objects/features, which can be of great interest to others.
7. Have students change partners and change roles.
8. Ask them to write a description/narration paper about their special rooms, which should be very vivid in their minds.
9. As a follow-up, students can read, critique, and comment on each other's papers.

References and Further Reading

Byram, M. (1989). *Cultural studies in foreign language education.* Clevedon, England: Multilingual Matters.

Contributors

Elizabeth Lange and Jong-oe Park have taught students of many different cultural and language backgrounds. Lange is presently teaching college students at Temple University Japan, in Tokyo, and Park has taught in both Korea and Japan.

Every Picture is Worth 1,000 Words

Levels
Intermediate +

Aims
Experience an event in the target culture
Practice language related to photographing that event

Class Time
30-45 minutes

Preparation Time
10-20 minutes

Resources
Picture of an anniversary cake or a lakeside picnic area

This activity allows creativity with a specific situation in the target culture.

Procedure

1. Briefly explain the custom of 25th, 50th, and 75th wedding anniversary celebrations in the United States. Show pictures if desired.
2. Read the following situation aloud:

   Helen and Herb O'Hara are going to have a 50th anniversary party at a picnic ground in the lakeside park in their small town. It's a beautiful place with a beach, a playground, and boats to rent. They are going to have 100 guests.

3. Brainstorm with the class, and sketch on the blackboard when necessary, the various objects, food items, and activities that might be part of this anniversary celebration but that also might be new vocabulary for the students, such as *docks, rafts, canoes, rowboats, swings, slides, picnic tables, barbecue grills, casseroles, kegs of beer, horseshoes,* and so on.
4. Put the students into groups of three and give them the following instructions:

   Your group has been hired as a team to take photographs for this event. Decide exactly what pictures you will take—where they will be taken, who will be in them, and so on. Among the guests there are Helen and Herb's two sons and two daughters, as well as 16 grandchildren. You may take only 20 pictures, and Helen and Herb have asked that you be as creative as possible in your picture dialogue.

148

Write on the blackboard: 2 sons, 2 daughters, 16 grandchildren, and 20 shots.

5. Have students choose one member of their group to take notes and list the pictures. When finished, have students choose their most creative photo idea and either describe it to the rest of the class, or draw a picture of it on the board and explain it.

Caveats and Options

1. An alternative to having each group share its best shot with the class is to ask each group to put its list of photos on the board and compare the various choices, noting both the similarities among all the groups and the most creative ideas.
2. Another alternative, especially for a more advanced group, is to have the picnic at an amusement park or theme park picnic ground. Several photographs of such parks would probably be necessary for vocabulary in this case.

Contributor

Victoria Holder, ESL instructor at San Francisco State University and San Francisco City College, in the United States, has recently published a teacher's resource book on practicing grammar without paper.

Weekly Entertainment Guides: Painting Your Town Read

Levels
Beginning +

Aims
Learn about social and recreational behavior in U.S. contemporary culture
Read U.S. newspapers
Stimulate discussion comparing social and cultural behavior in the United States and home countries

Class Time
Two sessions of 1 hour each

Preparation Time
1 hour

Resources
Copy of weekly entertainment section in local newspaper
Handout

Toward the end of the work week, many newspapers contain a weekly entertainment insert (EI). The insert contains movie listings and reviews; new video releases; nightclub publicity; times and places of local live music performances; coverage of cultural, educational, recreational, and civic events; and advertisements. Special editions of the EI appear to highlight holidays such as Christmas and St. Valentine's Day. In the ESL context, the primary goals for using the EI as a classroom text are to give learners readings containing local and current information in a simple and visually supported format and heighten learners' awareness of the social and cultural ambiance in which they are currently living (to encourage them to participate in the social scene).

In an EFL context, the goals are to provide students with authentic and contemporary reading material concerning U.S. culture and activate conversation on high interest topics related to social, cultural, and recreational pastimes of U.S. peers.

Procedure

1. Arrange students into seated groups of four to five.
2. Give each group or each group member a copy of the same entertainment insert (e.g., "Valentine's Day" issue), and allow necessary time for all to skim and read EI (you may want to let them take it home).
3. Distribute handout with the following instructions:

First Group Session (1 hour)

- Assume that you will take a friend out for a social evening. You have US$60 to spend on the evening's entertainment, including dinner for two and a cinema, music, theatrical, or sports event (admission for two).
- Read the EI and its advertisements, noting activities of possible interest to you and your friend. Write down names and locations of restaurants and activities of interest. Include time of activities and information on advance ticket purchases and other relevant information.
- Cut out advertisements and discount coupons (e.g., two dinners for the price of one). Paste or display clipped information on one side of a sheet of paper.

Note to instructor: Discuss information for purpose of clarifying new vocabulary, comprehending nature of advertised events, prices, and so on.

Second Group Session (1 hour)

- Outline aloud and discuss your plans for the evening's events including times, places, costs, and reasons for choosing each activity.
- Question and assist your fellow presenters; ask about transportation, tipping, reasons for selecting events, dress, overall costs, and the like.
- (Optional) Make a small poster displaying clippings containing information about one group member's evening's plans, including schedule, location, prices, and other pertinent information.

Note to instructor: When the group presentations are finished, ask each group to select one "model" date for oral presentation to entire class (3 minutes each).

Caveats and Options

1. If the EI contains personal ads, groups may discuss meaning of selected advertisements (including abbreviations such as *SWM*) or ads of special interest to individual group members. Learning tasks may include writing one's own advertisement.
2. Holiday or special events EIs are very useful. For example, St. Valentine's Day issues contain classified "love notes" and special prices on couples' dinners, flowers, and gifts.
3. Students may find advertisements that are difficult to comprehend. Select these ads for discussion or display (e.g., *head cleaning* at a video repair store).
4. EIs may contain a map of the community, indicating locations of major advertisers' establishments (e.g., restaurants). This is very useful in determining travel time between events, proximity of events to each other, or needs for transportation.

Contributor

Frederick Jenks is professor and coordinator of multilingual-multicultural education and also director of the Center for Intensive English Studies at Florida State University in Tallahassee, Florida, in the United States.

Hand(y) Language

Levels
Any

Aims
Gain awareness of the communicative use of hand gestures in the target culture
Foster cross-cultural discussion on the relation of hand gestures to what they signify

Class Time
15 minutes

Preparation Time
5 minutes

Resources
Handout with pictures of person gesturing

Caveats and Options

This activity encourages learners to explore the extralinguistic component of the target culture and to promote cross-cultural understanding and comparison. Their importance is not only to enhance communication but also to develop students' awareness about how gestures contribute to understanding. Gestures are also important to explore because sometimes a gesture that is innocuous in one culture may be offensive in another.

Procedure

1. Pass out a handout with pictures of a person gesturing. If this is impractical, someone can mime the gestures or you can draw them on the chalkboard.
2. Tell them these are gestures used in the target culture (in this case U.S.).
3. Ask students to note what they think each gesture signifies.
4. Have them compare their guesses with other students.
5. If necessary, give them the correct answers.
6. Discuss and compare with students hand gestures in the students' own cultures. If possible, look into why a particular gesture has a particular meaning.

1. Students could be assigned to observe people in (or films of) the target culture and list what they think are hand gestures and what their specific meanings are. They could report their findings to the class for discussion.
2. With great care, the procedure could be extended to cover some hand gestures that should be avoided (rude or obscene ones) in the target culture.

Appendix: Sample Gestures Handout

What is he using his hands to "say"? If you think you know, write the answer in the appropriate blank. Even if you are not sure, try to guess.

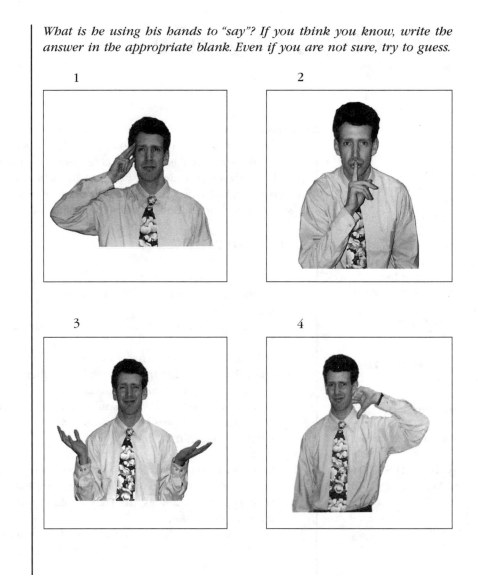

1

2

3

4

1. _____

2. _____

3. _____

4. _____

5. _____

6. _____

Contributor

Richard Humphries is a lecturer at Kansai Gaidai College, Hotani campus, in Hirakata City, Japan.

Cartoon Culture

Levels
Intermediate +

Aims
Learn to view cartoons
as culture learning tools
Learn conversational
vocabulary and grammar
Develop understanding
of target culture values
and humor

Class Time
1 hour

Preparation Time
20 minutes

Resources
Photocopies of one
comic strip, with and
without the dialogue
captions

Students are often frustrated by their inability to understand the target culture, especially its humor. Comic strips offer humorous materials that comment upon the culture. In this activity, students learn both culture and language as they work at understanding the humor, vocabulary, and grammar used in a particular comic strip and the values reflected within.

Procedure

1. Select a comic strip that you like because of how it reflects some aspect of the culture your students are studying.
2. Photocopy the cartoon, making one copy for every two students.
3. Take one copy and cover over all the dialogue that the characters say or think.
4. Photocopy this wordless cartoon, one for every two students. (You should now have two copies of the cartoon, one with words and one without, for each pair of students.)
5. In class, give pairs of students a copy of the wordless cartoon and have them write dialogue to match the picture, filling in the bubbles.
6. When dialogues have been written, have students look at each other's cartoons.
7. Ask the class to identify the most common interpretation of the cartoon and other possible interpretations as well. Encourage discussion of the factors that influenced the dialogues. Lead students to see that they wrote dialogue that reflected their own values and attitudes.
8. Give pairs of students a copy of the comic with the original script.
9. Have students identify the main message of the comic. Have them identify the actions and reactions of the characters in the strip.

10. In groups of three or four (two of the original pairs together), have students discuss why each character makes his or her statements and what else may have caused the character to feel or react in the way he or she did.
11. Have the groups discuss what values or attitudes this comic strip reflects.
12. Have each group report its conclusions to the class.
13. Finish the activity with teacher comments about the appropriateness of the conclusions.

Caveats and Options

1. Step 9 may also involve a vocabulary or grammar explanation. You could wait for students to ask, or teach quickly before the students begin to analyze the message. Alternatively, explain briefly only if asked and do a more complex study of the grammar if you feel it useful at a later time.
2. Students may have difficulty coming to the conclusions that you would like. Be prepared for this eventuality by analyzing the comic yourself ahead of time and by inserting suggestions if students seem off track during their group discussions.
3. After having done the above activity once or twice, students could read the comics for homework and bring one that they are interested in to class.
4. Students could be asked to do this kind of analysis as homework and to journal about their interpretations and conclusions.

References and Further Reading

Chan, D., Kaplan-Weinger, J., & Sandstrom, D. (1995). *Journeys to cultural understanding.* Boston: Heinle & Heinle.

Contributors

Deborah Sandstrom teaches linguistics and TESL at the University of Chicago, and Judith Kaplan-Weinger and Debra Chan teach linguistics and TESL at Northeastern Illinois University, in the United States.

Meeyauu! Does Your Cat Speak English?

Levels
Any

Aims
Learn the vowel sounds
of English
Give examples of words
in the home languages
that contain the same
sounds
Compare animal sounds
from a cultural point of
view

Class Time
2-3 hours

Preparation Time
1 hour

Resources
Pictures of various
animals commonly
known to the group
Sample vowel chart
handout
Handout of animal
sounds

Procedure

1. Show pictures of animals and ask students to determine the sounds associated with each animal (e.g., cats purr, *meeyau*). Pair or group students so that various cultures are represented and ask them to give sounds associated with each animal. Debrief and share answers as a group, noting cultural differences.

2. Focus on cats and ask the students to be aware of the shapes of their mouths and their jaw position when saying *meeyau* aloud. Ask the students to tell you what happens to the mouth (spread, then rounded) and to the jaw (closed, then open). Ask them to consider, as well, where the sound seems to be coming from. Does it come from the front of the mouth or from the throat? Explain that the changes in mouth and jaw result in the various English vowels. Introduce the terms *round, spread* (shape of lips), *high, low* (jaw opening), and *front, back* (sound location).

3. Provide students with a handout containing a vowel chart with vowels missing and with words containing the vowels listed below the chart (see Appendix).

4. Guide students to fill in the vowel chart and to describe each vowel according to the descriptors: round/spread, high/low, front/central/back.

5. Say each vowel and ask the students to decide which word contains that vowel. Make sure students have filled in their charts accurately.

6. Ask the students to list one word from their home language that also contains each vowel. Warn that they may not have that sound in their language, so some may be left blank.

7. Compare answers, listing words and meanings on a master chart or transparency to be compiled, then distributed to the entire class.

Caveats and Options

1. As an extension to Step 1, you could sing "Old MacDonald Had a Farm," and, when giving the sound for each animal, call out "American sound," "Malaysian sound," "Mexican sound," when referring to what a goat sounds like, for example. This would be appropriate for young learners.

2. As a cultural-focus follow-up to Step 1, you may also wish to discuss the roles of various animals in the societies represented and whether the animal is a pet, a helpmate, or a food source. Some examples:
   - Chinese societies often have tea houses where men bring their pet songbirds to sing together.
   - The Chinese enjoy having goldfish ponds as the goldfish is a symbol of wealth and prosperity.
   - Many Americans value dogs as pets and as hunting companions, whereas in New Zealand, they help to herd sheep.
   - Muslims often consider dogs as very dirty animals while in Korea, it is not uncommon to eat dogs.

3. As a supplement to Step 2, you may wish to ask students to bring a mirror to class so they can watch the mouth and jaw as they "talk like a cat."

4. As an alternative to Step 6, ask that they think of another English word that uses that same vowel sound (rather than a word from their home language).

5. As an extension to review, use vowel information while building dictionary skills. Ask students to look at the vowel symbols used in dic-tionaries and to identify those they have learned. With intermediate and advanced learners, you may wish to focus on one or two vowels a week. Review the descriptors, then ask students to find a new English word in the dictionary that includes that focus vowel. Students should be able to write the new word properly, correctly underline the vowel sound targeted, and use the dictionary pronunciation guide to pronounce the word correctly.

6. Note that these activities can be adapted to various target languages, substituting Spanish vowels, for example, when teaching the vowel chart and vowel descriptors.

References and Further Reading

Yule, G. (1982). *Language files*. Reynoldsburg, OH: Department of Linguistics, The Ohio State University/Advocate Publishing Group.

Yule, G. (1985). *The study of language*. Cambridge: Cambridge University Press.

Appendix

Handout: Sample Vowel Chart

Directions:

1. Fill in the English words that follow, putting each in the proper blank. The first one is done for you.

bat	bait	bit	bought
boat	but	bet	boot
book	bother		

2. Think of a word in your own language that has the same sound. Write it on the blank labeled *yours*.

	Front (spread)	Central	Back (rounded)
High	i _beat_ (English) _____ (yours)		u _____ (English) _____ (yours)
	I _____ (English) _____ (yours)		U _____ (English) _____ (yours)
Mid	e _____ (English) _____ (yours)	_____ (English) _____ (yours)	o _____ (English) _____ (yours)
	E _____ (English) _____ (yours)		_____ (English) _____ (yours)
Low	æ _____ (English) _____ (yours)	a _____ (English) _____ (yours)	

Key to English words:

i =	beat		u =	boot
I =	bit		U =	book
e =	bait	ə = but	o =	boat
E =	bet		ɔ =	bought
æ =	bat	a = bother		

Contributor

Kim Hughes Wilhelm is curriculum coordinator for the Center for English as a Second Language and assistant professor of linguistics, Southern Illinois University at Carbondale, in the United States.

Part V: Activities for Intercultural Exploration

My Ideal Classroom

Levels
Intermediate +

Aim
Contrast and compare
differences in student
and teacher assumptions
of appropriate
classroom behavior,
interactions, and
environment

Class Time
1 hour

Preparation Time
15 minutes

Resources
Newsprint and markers

This activity explores beliefs and assumptions held by different cultures of appropriate classroom behavior, interactions, and environment. Many students come from countries where the classroom environment is completely opposite from that encouraged for promoting communicative competence. This demonstrates that the concept of *classroom* is not universal and can be the beginning of helping students adjust to the different expectations of the communicative classroom.

Procedure

1. For homework or in class have students describe their ideal class-room using the following categories: teacher, students, environment, teacher/student interactions, and student/student interactions.
2. Have ready to share with students your own responses, those of a typical teacher or students in a communicative classroom, or both.
3. In pairs have students compare their work.
4. Combine two pairs and have them put their responses on newsprint.
5. Post all the newsprint posters at the front and have students look at them for major similarities and major differences. Highlight these.
6. Contrast student responses and compare with yours.
7. In small groups have students discuss the following:
   - Which contrasts will be most difficult/easiest to adjust to?
   - How can they ease their adjustment?
   - What can the teacher do to help? What can other students do?

Caveats and Options

1. This is also a useful exercise for teacher training programs to demonstrate the vast cultural differences that teachers and students can have regarding classroom behavior and the general classroom environment.

2. Making the transition from a traditional classroom to one promoting communicative competence is very risky for students and takes time. In some cases, a total transition will not be appropriate.

References and Further Reading

Althen, G. (Ed.). (1994). *Learning across cultures* (2nd ed.). Washington, DC: NAFSA: Association of International Educators. (Also available through Intercultural Press)

Brislin, R., & Yoshida, T. (1994). *Intercultural communication training: An introduction.* Thousand Oaks, CA: Sage.

Brislin, R., Cushner, K., Cherrie, C., & Yong, M. (1986). *Intercultural interactions*. Beverly Hills, CA: Sage.

Byrd, P. (Ed.). (1986). *Teaching across cultures in the university ESL program.* Washington, DC: NAFSA.

Gaston, J. (1984). *Cultural awareness teaching techniques.* Brattleboro, VT: Pro Lingua Associates.

Gudykunst, W., & Kim, Y. (1992). *Communicating with strangers: An approach to intercultural communication* (2nd ed.). New York: McGraw-Hill.

Hofstede, G. (1986). Cultural differences in teaching and learning. *International Journal of Intercultural Relations, 1, 10,* 301–320.

Hofstede, G. (1991). *Cultures and organizations: Software of the mind.* London: McGraw-Hill.

Valdes, J. (Ed.). (1986). *Culture bound: Bridging the cultural gap in language teaching.* New York: Cambridge University Press.

Wurzel, J., & Fischman, N. (Producers). (1993). *A different place: The intercultural classroom* [Video]. Newtonville, MA: Intercultural Resource Corporation. (Also available through Intercultural Press)

Contributor

Carolyn Ryffel is an independent consultant specializing in intercultural communication, foreign language training (ESL, Spanish, German), and cross-cultural training. She lives in Arlington, Virginia, in the United States.

Getting-to-Know-You Posters

Levels
Intermediate +

Aims
Become acquainted
with classmates
Share cultural
experiences on the first
day of class

Class Time
45–60 minutes

Preparation Time
None

Resources
Polaroid camera and
film, brown paper,
markers, scissors, glue

This activity explores student-generated posters in a vibrant and challenging manner, revealing diverse interests and backgrounds, and enhancing oral communication and intercultural awareness.

Procedure

1. Tell your students they will be creating posters about themselves and that this will include a photo and brief text.
2. Brainstorm with the class some of the personal information they might include: name, age, hobbies, interests, and learning objectives. As for intercultural information, they should mention place of origin, cultures, and languages they have had contact with; cultures they are interested in; and their own travels, whether in their own countries or overseas. List these points on the board.
3. Have the students take pictures of each other with the Polaroid. Do not forget to include yourself in this process—your poster can be an interesting source of information on the target culture.
4. Once the pictures have been taken, have students paste their photos on big pieces of brown paper and organize their text however they want. Make sure colored markers are available.
5. As soon as the posters are ready, post them round the classroom. Encourage students to walk around, comparing and contrasting experiences.
6. As a final wrap-up, walk together from poster to poster, making sure that final questions are addressed and that everyone has a chance to clarify any extra bit of information. Take note of issues that could be addressed later on in the course.
7. Leave these posters on the walls for a couple of weeks, or as long as you feel is necessary.

Caveats and Options

1. A similar procedure can be used at different moments of the program, when focusing on other cross-cultural experiences, for example, food, artifacts, clothing, field trips, interviewees—in fact, whatever project the group is involved in.
2. If you happen to have a monocultural class, have students include family background (a couple of generations back), and which area/city/village they are originally from. Have students discuss their cultural references.

Contributor

Carla Reichmann, a graduate of the MAT program at the School for International Training, Brattleboro, Vermont, has lived in the United States, Brazil, and Israel and is a teacher of ESOL.

Exploring Cross-Cultural Miscommunication

Levels
Intermediate +

Aims
Become aware of how
cultural assumptions in
everyday situations can
lead to cross-cultural
miscommunication
Develop vocabulary to
describe cultural situations
and the miscommuni-
cation that can result

Class Time
Two class sessions, several
days apart
50 minutes, first day;
20 minutes, second day

Preparation Time
35 minutes

Resources
Students who are cur-
rently living overseas,
preferably away from their
native culture for the first
time
Teacher who is knowl-
edgeable and experienced
in the host culture, not
necessarily a native
Pencil, paper

This activity asks students to write a description of a situation they have experienced with a native of the host culture, one that resulted in cross-cultural miscommunication. In order to familiarize students with what is expected, it is a good idea to present examples of such situations beforehand (see Appendix for a sample cultural episode, and References for collections of cultural episodes).

Procedure

1. Select several cultural episodes that could be interesting to or relevant for your students (e.g., episodes that involve social interaction with members of the host culture, or educational situations).
2. Photocopy the descriptions of the episodes separate from the possible interpretations and separate from the explanations. Or, alternately, make overhead transparencies for a class reading of the episodes.
3. Read through the description of the episode with students. Explain any vocabulary words students may not be familiar with. Ask students if they have experienced such a situation in the host culture, and how they felt about it.
4. After students have discussed the content of the episode, hand out copies or project the transparencies of the possible interpretations of the incident. Ask students which interpretation they would choose and why, based on their cultural assumptions.
5. Offer your opinion about the most appropriate interpretation of the situation, based on the cultural assumptions of the host culture.
6. When discussion of the possible interpretations has run its course, provide copies or the overhead of the explanations of the possible interpretations. Have students discuss the differences between what

is considered appropriate behavior in their native culture and in the host culture, using the cultural episode as an example.

7. Repeat this procedure once or twice, depending on the interest of the students, and the amount of time available.

8. Divide students, preferably of the same cultural background, into small groups. Ask them to write a description of a situation that one or more of them experienced in the host culture and that resulted in a cross-cultural misunderstanding.

9. Have students complete the description of the cultural episode, and provide several possible interpretations of the incident for homework due in several days. Although students do not have to explain their interpretations, they should be ready to discuss the most appropriate interpretation of the incident, based on the cultural assumptions of the host culture. Encourage students to seek out natives or informants of the host culture, for assistance in correctly interpreting the situation from their perspective.

10. When students have finished writing their cultural episodes, arrange students from two groups into a circle, with the students from the two groups facing each other. Have the groups exchange their cultural episodes, and read the episode of the other group, as well as the possible interpretations. Students should discuss their interpretations of each of the situations, and the differences between the cultural assumptions of the native culture and their host culture.

Caveats and Options

1. As a follow-up activity, students should be encouraged to develop their own strategies for interpreting and responding appropriately in cross-cultural situations, to reduce the potential for cross-cultural miscommunication. For example, students could talk with the other person about what has gone wrong when there has been a misunderstanding.

References and Further Reading

Brislin, R. W., Cushner, K., Cherrie, C., & Yong, M. (1986). *Intercultural interactions: A practical guide*. Newbury Park, CA: Sage.

Dindi, H., Gazur, M., Gazur, W. M., & Kirkkopru-Dindi, A. (1989). *Turkish culture for Americans*. Boulder, CO: International Concepts.

Appendix: Sample Description of a Cultural Episode and Follow-Up

Part 1: The Episode

Susan had recently been hired as a lecturer to teach English and cultural studies in the American Studies Department at the University of Munich. She had a master's in TESOL and was currently working on her dissertation for a doctorate in Second Languages and Cultures Education from a major American university. She was very excited about her new position and the opportunity to live overseas for the first time in 10 years. Susan had minored in German at the undergraduate level and had lived in Germany as a college student on a semester abroad program. She was relatively fluent in the language, and thought she understood the intricacies of German culture well enough to adapt easily to her new environment.

After only a week or so on the job, a professor called her into his office. She had never met him before and was not sure who he was. He asked her to sit down and briefly asked about her family. Then, he told her he was giving a talk on Mark Twain in a few days and wanted her to look over his presentation. The paper was currently being typed, but would be ready shortly. He would need the corrected copy back the next day.

Susan was taken aback by the directness of his request, which had not been accompanied by any kind of politeness expression. He did not apologize for such short notice, or even ask if she had the time to do this for him. Nor did he express any appreciation when she said she would be happy to do it. She was also confused about what exactly she was supposed to do: respond to the content and organization of the paper or correct his grammatical errors. When she asked for clarification, he seemed to grow impatient and got up, a clear indication it was time for her to leave.

As she was leaving the office, she made reference to a presentation she was currently working on for the Amerika-Haus, which would have to be translated into German. Perhaps he could help her with that. After all, she said cheerfully and at the time quite innocently, "I guess you owe me one."

The professor was incensed at her comment and turned bright red. He never gave her the paper to look over. Susan sensed that their first encounter had gone terribly wrong. Even after an apology on her part, relations turned from bad to worse.

What had gone wrong?

Part 2: Possible Interpretations

1. Germans do not use politeness expressions when they are making requests.
2. As a woman, Susan was viewed as subordinate to the men in the department, and was, therefore, subject to being asked to fulfill secretarial responsibilities.
3. As a lecturer, Susan was not equal to a professor. The remark she made as she was leaving his office suggested they were colleagues of equal status. In the hierarchy of a German university, she was clearly his subordinate.
4. Susan's contract stated that she was to teach six courses a semester, as well as fulfill any other duties expected of her. Correcting professors' papers was expected of her, and was, therefore, part of her job responsibilities.

Part 3: Explanations

1. German includes many politeness expressions. On the other hand, sociolinguistic conventions regarding their usage differs from American English. For example, it would not be expected that someone at a higher level would use politeness expressions with someone at a lower level. However, there is another more fundamental explanation. Please choose again.
2. Women in Germany enjoy greater equality in society than in the United States, although the percentage of female professors at the university level is much lower than in the States. However, this particular department had a reputation for its openness towards women. Please choose again.
3. Professors in Germany hold a sacred position in society, and any affront to their privileged status is taken with the utmost seriousness. Moreover, German universities are much less egalitarian than in the States. Such requests of subordinates are common from professors, and lecturers who are looking to make an academic career for themselves understand what is expected of them. This is the correct answer.

4. Susan's contract did include additional responsibilities, such as library duty. However, she had not been told by the director of the Institute that correcting professors' papers was part of those additional responsibilities and, therefore, was not prepared for such a request. To the contrary, the director had specifically said she would not be held responsible for working in the library. Indeed, her contract even specified that lecturers could be asked to teach up to seven courses, but the Institute only required their lecturers to teach six. Choose again.

Contributor

Susan Bosher has a PhD in Second Languages and Cultures Education from the University of Minnesota. She has taught overseas in Germany and Turkey.

Comparing Cultural Events

Levels
Any

Aims
Become aware of
different cultural
practices in different
cultures
Practice informal letter
writing skills

Class Time
1 hour

Preparation Time
5 minutes

Resources
5- to 10-minute segment
of film showing an
event such as a wedding
or a funeral that is
culturally embedded in
the target language

S tudents often lack the confidence to engage in conversation or practice their language skills with native speakers of the target language. One of the reasons for this is a fear of not knowing how to act. This activity enables students to discuss the issue of cultural differences. A better understanding of the target language culture will promote interest and increase motivation for learning the language.

Procedure

1. Select a short film clip that shows a cultural event such as a dinner party, a birthday party, or holiday celebrations.
2. Give students the chart in the Appendix and ask them to complete the first column while watching the clip.
3. After viewing, ask the students in groups to discuss what takes place in their culture. Have them complete the last column of the chart.
4. Ask students to imagine they are living in the target culture environment, and having attended the event shown in the film clip, they decide to write a letter to a friend telling him about the event.

Caveats and Options

1. The activity leads nicely into project work. Ask the students, in groups, to find additional materials about the cultural event (e.g., pictures, photographs, articles, clothes).
2. If you have available space in the classroom the students can design a "cultural wall" to display their work and materials.
3. A cultural library is an effective way of storing students' work. Ensure that it is accessible to other students and teachers in the school who may be interested in finding out about different cultural habits.

4. To fully understand the different cultural approaches to an event, students could perform a short role play.
5. In a multilingual class, ask each group of students to talk about, or more formally, give a presentation about the cultural event. In a monolingual or a low-level ESOL class, one group of students could present the cultural event each week.

Appendix: Sample Chart

Name of Event: _____

Country of Origin: _____   Student's Country: _____

Where is the event taking place?

_____

Who or what is involved?

_____

Column 1	Column 2

What is happening?

_____	_____
_____	_____
_____	_____
_____	_____
_____	_____

Contributor

Susan Fitzgerald is an EFL instructor at the Department of English, Hong Kong Polytechnic University in Kowloon, Hong Kong.

Culture Shocks

Levels
Advanced

Aims
Understand cultural differences, especially those with potential for provoking shocking reactions
Practice the language associated with reactions such as shock and surprise

Class Time
1 hour

Preparation Time
5 minutes

Resources
None

A Steven Spielberg movie, *Indiana Jones and the Temple of Doom,* showed an exotic table setting covered with sumptuous food, which the Western guests were anticipating with delight only to discover, when lifting a lid, monkey brains piled up steaming hot under it. Similarly, this activity generates shocking or surprising cross-cultural incidents to help students learn how to express this surprise through language.

Procedure

1. Give a number of examples of how you were surprised at the way things were done in another culture—events that made you more aware of your own cultural values, such as your astonishment at people slurping noodles and your alarm (quite often accompanied by screams) at seeing a whole fish (with its eyes staring up at you) on a plate, and if you were given a gift (e.g., a luxury for the giver but horrifying to receiver—a silkworm to eat—how you might react and why).

2. Also, practice some of the language that will help the students to express their reactions and how to explain their cultural points of view.

3. Ask each student to think of a situation in which they experienced or observed someone else going through an unusual emotional experience deriving from cultural differences and write the situation down on a piece of paper. (Make sure that they maintain a neutral stance in their description.)

4. Then, in rotating pairs, have students interview a number of people and take notes, asking them what their reaction would be in that situation and why.

5. After students summarize their findings on real and possible reactions as related to actual or imaginary experiences in different cultures, conclude the activity by comparing and contrasting what are considered rude/tactful/polite reactions and the different effects they have on people of other cultures. The whole purpose here is to sensitize the students to other cultures, thus building pragmatic competence.

References and Further Reading

Thomas, J. (1983). Cross-cultural pragmatic failure. *Applied Linguistics, 4,* 91–111.

Valdes, J. M. (Ed.). (1986). *Culture bound*. New York: Cambridge University Press.

Contributors

Elizabeth Lange and Jong-oe Park have taught students of many different cultural and language backgrounds. Lange is presently teaching college students in Japan. Jong-oe Park has taught English to college students and adults in South Korea and Japan.

Name That Country

Levels
High intermediate +

Aims
Learn about world
cultures by using
previous knowledge and
in-class resources
Practice scanning and
research skills

Class Time
1–2 hours

Preparation Time
30 minutes if
Culturgrams available;
otherwise 1–2 hours

Resources
Country fact sheet,
minus name of country
Information gleaned
from books, texts,
encyclopedias, or
Culturgrams

This is an enjoyable problem-solving activity that gets students to test their knowledge of other cultures by working with another student to figure out which country/culture their fact sheet describes. If this activity takes place at the end of the course, they might be able to decide on the answer based on what they remember from the course. If it comes at the beginning, it could serve as an introduction to the cultures that will be discussed throughout the course as well as to increase their awareness of cultural differences.

Procedure

1. Using *Culturgrams* (see References and Further Reading) or information gleaned from other sources, create cultural fact sheets for various countries. List approximately 10 facts or descriptions. Along with cultural information, also give information on geography or climate to serve as clues to general location. Do not write the name of the country or culture described or its exact location on the fact sheet. Label the sheets "1-2-3" or "A-B-C" and keep an answer sheet listing the corresponding country names.

2. Distribute fact sheets so that two students have the same handout (i.e., if you have 20 students, you will cover 10 countries).

3. Instruct students to walk around the room and try to find the student that has the same sheet as they do by asking fellow students yes/no questions (e.g., *Is it impolite in your country for the bottom of one's foot to point at another person? Is most of your country a dry and arid desert?*). They should not show the other students their sheet until they get at least six questions answered.

4. After they have determined that they have found their partner, they should try to find out which country they have, based on previous class discussions, handouts, texts, encyclopedias, or *Culturgrams*.

5. After everyone has had ample time to determine (or guess) which country they have, they can share their answers with the class and tell the class about that country. There can also be a class discussion on the strategies they used to pinpoint the country, or why they got an incorrect answer (e.g., *Is the country they chose similar in culture, climate, religion, and so on to the country they should have chosen?*).

Caveats and Options

1. Give students the opportunity to generate the fact sheets on their own based on the culture, climate, and the like of their own country and use these as a basis for the activity.

2. This can be turned into a writing project on the culture of the country the students were working with or of some other country that was discussed.

3. This activity can be done as a competition to see which pair can finish first.

4. If the activity ends earlier than planned, the students could record their guesses and then exchange papers with another pair, trying to guess which country it is.

5. The individual clues could be used as the answers in a *Jeopardy-*style game.

References and Further Reading

Brigham Young University. (1991). *Culturgram for the '90s.* Provo, UT: David M. Kennedy Center for International Studies.

Appendix: Fact Sheet on Egypt[*]

1. Social status is important in this society, so the conversational gambits for greetings reflect awareness of social class.
2. The people of this country like to offer guests elegant and costly meals.
3. In this country, men and women do not have physical contact in public, with the exception of married or engaged couples who may walk arm in arm.
4. In this country, one neither displays the bottom of one's feet to another person nor rests one's feet on a table or chair in the company of others.
5. Most women in this country conceal their hair and most of their bodies (except their faces and hands) in loose-fitting garments.
6. This country's dedication to the cultural arts is internationally recognized; films and television programming are particularly notable.
7. Most of the population of this country is currently Muslim; however, it was among the first nations visited by the apostle Mark and Christianized within three centuries.
8. Wealthy inhabitants of this country socialize in private clubs; men of other classes congregate in coffee shops.
9. Extended families may live together in close quarters in this country.
10. The people of this country are considered humorous, demonstrative, and impassioned.

Contributors

Rebecca Sherbahn and Stephanie Allomong are master's degree candidates in Applied Linguistics/ESL at Georgia State University, in the United States.

[*]Adapted from *Culturgram for the '90s: Arab Republic of Egypt* (1991).

Culture Quest

Levels
Intermediate +

Aims
Focus on own culture
and explain it to
classmates
Learn more about the
target language culture
and each other's
cultures

Class Time
50 minutes

Preparation Time
2½ hours first time only

Resources
Game boards, game
pieces, dice

In an informal but competitive way, students will learn about each other's and the target language culture. The questions in the activity cover the kinds of situations in which cultures have been shown to differ.

Procedure

1. Divide the class into groups of three to six students.
2. Give each group a game board (see Appendix for sample) and have them sit round the board at a table or on the floor.
3. Give each student a game piece and each group a die. The student who rolls the highest number on the die begins the game.
4. Suggest that students take turns in a clockwise direction.
5. Each of the board's squares contains a question asking the students to share something about their culture. Some squares are marked "make a question." In this case, have the student ask a question about the culture of the person whose turn is next.
6. End the game when one of the participants gets to the finish or when all of them get there.
7. Encourage students to ask clarification or vocabulary questions whenever necessary.
8. When the game is over, bring the students back to the large group to process the content of their culture quest. Ask the groups to share some interesting observations and comment on what they have learned about culture in general and about different cultures.

Caveats and Options

1. Vary the questions to relate to the specific goals of the lesson or the course.

2. Precede the activity with a general discussion about culture. You may distinguish between observations and judgments, that is, between a neutral account of what someone has observed and a culturally biased perspective on those observations.

3. Encourage students to act out the answer to a particular question involving the other group members in the demonstration.

References and Further Reading

Althen, G. (1988). *American ways: A guide for foreigners in the United States*. Yarmouth, ME: Intercultural Press.

Samovar, L. A., & Porter, R. E. (1991). *Intercultural communication: A reader*. Belmont, CA: Wadsworth.

Appendix: Sample Game Board

Culture Quest

					START
You win a turn!	Do you tip? Who do you tip?	What gestures of good luck do you use?	Name some conversation taboos		
Do you shake hands? When? How do you do it?			Do you give compliments? When and to whom?		How many times do you extend invitations and offers?
What are you expected to do when you receive a present?	**LET US SHARE**		How do you greet friends verbally and nonverbally?		When do you make/avoid eye contact?
Would you challenge your teachers if they made an error?			FINISH		What is your concept of arriving on time? Give examples.
How do you get a waiter's attention?					How do you address your instructors/ supervisors?
Make a question	Do you have any super-stitions?	What do you joke about?	How do you form a line while waiting?	Make a question	Do you share when you bring a snack to school/ work?

Contributors

Elka Todeva is a faculty member of the MAT Program of the School for International Training in Brattleboro, Vermont, in the United States. Milena Savova teaches at the College of Staten Island/City University of New York, in the United States.

The Hakone Encounter

This activity offers students an opportunity to interact with different culture informants while working with "culture cards." Each culture card contains a statement about a practice in a different culture. Students will formulate appropriate questions to elicit additional information about practices that interest them. Informants (from the teaching staff, community, or both) answer the questions by explaining the reasons for these practices and facilitating a discussion about how values (as seen in the practices) are manifested similarly or differently by people from different cultures. The discussion can include a focus on comparing and contrasting both the target culture and the culture of the participants.

Procedure

1. Prior to this activity, have informants/facilitators prepare three or four cards listing practices that occur in their cultures. Put only one practice on each card. Ask that they write the practice as an objective account of what any observer would see or hear. Be sure they put the country name on the card as well (see Appendix).

2. Introduce the activity by telling students that they will practice asking and answering questions about culture. The topics of discussion will be the cultures of the informants in their group.

3. Ask participants to be aware of the following questions during their discussions:
   - What am I learning about the different cultures?
   - What similarities and differences do I recognize?
   - Why are there similarities and differences?

4. Explain that the facilitators in each group will show them three or four cards that contain observations about practices in the informants' culture(s). Tell them to choose a card that they are interested in and to ask the informant questions about it.

5. Divide students into three or four groups.

6. Assign an informant and his or her corresponding culture cards to each group.

7. Begin the group activity by putting the culture cards on a table. Give students time to read the cards, ask vocabulary questions, and choose a card that interests them.

8. Distribute the Exchanging Cultural Information handout (see Appendix) to each student. Again allow students to read the handout and ask vocabulary questions.

9. Instruct students to use the language on the handout to formulate appropriate questions concerning practices that they want to inquire about.

10. Facilitate a lively discussion. Focus on the reasons behind the practices, highlight similarities as they come up, and point out that some differences occur in the way people interpret the same belief or value.

11. At the end of 30 minutes, ask each informant to stop the discussion and process their group's use of polite language by asking these questions:

  ● Which of the phrases in the handout did you use? Not use? Why?

  ● Can you give an example of an inappropriate question or behavior that would affect our discussion?

  ● What could be the reasons you sometimes forget to ask these questions politely?

12. After processing the use of polite language, form four new, mixed groups. Every new group should consist of students from each of the initial groups plus an informant.

13. For the final 20 minutes of this activity, process the content of their culture discussion. Ask each student to share what they discussed in the first group. Highlight and illustrate a point when the opportunity arises. Ask general and situational questions:

  ● What have you learned about culture in general? About different cultures?

  ● If you travel to a different country and experience something new or commit a cultural blunder, what would you do? What would your perspective be?

Caveats and Options

1. This activity works best in situations in which you can have one informant for every five to seven students.
2. The activity can be preceded by discussions about culture. A lesson on the difference between observations (objective or neutral accounts of what we see or hear) and judgments (value-laden opinions about our observations) will also help the activity.
3. An introduction or prior lesson on appropriate and inappropriate questions can also add value to the activity.
4. Informants should be good facilitators. They should feel comfortable talking about culture and should be able to guide students through discussions about culture.
5. If you have access to more informants, two per group work nicely.
6. If you only have informants from one culture, you can have them present practices about cultures in countries where they have lived.
7. When answering students' questions, refer to them questions about their own cultures, for example:
   - Do you have a corresponding practice in your culture?
   - I have observed an interesting practice in your culture that I don't understand. Do you mind if I ask you about it?
8. In-depth discussions about values and culture can be clearly illustrated by using the image of an iceberg: Sometimes, if you only see the practice (the above-the-water part of an iceberg), you forget about the underlying values that are not visible (the below-the-water part of the iceberg). What seems different or unknown?
9. When conducting the final discussion, present a specific situation. Ask how students might deal with a cultural blunder a foreigner might commit in their country.

References and Further Reading

Levine, D., Baxter, J., & McNulty, P. (1987). *The culture puzzle*. Englewood Cliffs, NJ: Prentice Hall.

Appendix

Acknowledgments

This activity was first used in the Business Program of the Language Institute of Japan. It is named after a weekend retreat held in Hakone, a mountainous region near Odawara. The activity was a prelude to having students explain their culture to the staff. We thank the various faculty who contributed to the development of this activity.

Handout 1: Exchanging Cultural Information

Asking About Other Cultures

Note: The italicized phrases are possible places or situations; any country or situation of interest could be substituted.

- I've noticed something I don't understand. May I ask you about it? Could you tell me why *no one corrected the teacher's mistake?*
- Is it OK if I *compliment a woman in my office?*
- Do you think it's OK to say, *"I completely disagree?"*
- In *Japan* people usually *bow when they greet someone.* What about *where you're from? In China?* Is it the same?
- Why is that done? Is that usual?
- Is there a special reason for doing that?

Explaining Your Own Culture or Customs

- In *Japan* people usually *give money as a wedding gift.*
- In my experience, *most people give about ¥ 50,000.*
- I'm not sure. I think it depends on *how well you know the family.*
- Some people from where I'm from might be uncomfortable *kissing in public.* It depends *on the person.*
- In my culture, I think *eating fish for breakfast* is relatively unusual.

Handout 2: Sample Culture Cards

Sample text for cards follows.

Philippines

In the countryside, the church bell will ring at 6:00 p.m., and the young people will go up to a senior citizen and put the older person's right hand on the younger person's forehead.

Japan

TV newscasters bow to the audience.

China

For wedding presents, we usually give an even number of things, not an odd number. For example six or eight tea cups, but never seven.

Contributors

Alberto Gabriel Carbonilla, Jr. is the program developer of the Language Institute of Japan, in Odawara, Kanagawa, Japan. Steve Cornwell is an instructor at Osaka Jogakuin Junior College in Osaka, Japan.

Three-Way Journal

Levels
Intermediate +

Aims
Involve parents and
other family members in
the educational
experience
Learn about own
culture
Write about, discuss,
and compare own and
target culture
Demonstrate writing
skills

Class Time
15-30 minutes

Preparation Time
1-2 hours

Resources
Journal notebooks for
each student

Sometimes young students from a variety of cultures have much to learn about their own culture as well as a target culture. To help facilitate this learning, a three-way dialogue journal between teacher, student, and parent, sibling, or other relative can result in many valuable cultural lessons.

Procedure

1. Choose a topic, for example: family life, beliefs behind ceremonies and traditions, educational practices, beliefs and attitudes about particular cultural topics.
2. Introduce the idea of a three-way dialogue journal and demonstrate.
3. Using the chosen topic, write to students individually in their journals, asking several questions and giving some information about the target culture.
4. Ask students to respond to the questions by writing in their journals.
5. Have students take their journals home to parents, older siblings, or other family members. They should respond with further information and direct questions to you.
6. Continue the dialogue. The interaction as well as wealth of cultural information should be gratifying.

Caveats and Options

1. This activity can be time consuming when you respond individually to all students, but it is worth it.
2. Choose 1 day of the week as journal day; that way students have the whole week to complete the exercise but can submit their work as

soon as they are ready. You can then respond as they come in, a few every day.

3. This is a very informative way to get to know your students.

4. The activity is useful for assessing the writing skills of students and determining which areas need work.

Contributor

Debbie Gassaway-Hayward works for International Organization for Migration in Kenya. She is the coordinator of cultural orientation and language training for African refugees resettling in the United States.

Keep Your Distance

Levels
Intermediate +

Aims
Expand awareness of
personal distance in
communication
encounters
Become more sensitive
to contextual factors
influencing the use of
personal space in the
target culture

Class Time
30 minutes

Preparation Time
5 minutes

Resources
Tape measure, chalk or
marker, chalkboard

This activity gives learners a chance to experience their use of interpersonal distances in a given communication setting. The demonstration serves as a basis for discussing the nature of proxemics for intercultural exploration.

Procedure

1. Choose two female students and give them a hypothetical situation such as running into each other on a street and then chatting about an event familiar to both of them. Have them approach each other and begin talking in front of the class. The rest of the class will be observing the participants' behavior. Do not tell the actors that this task is about the use of personal space to make sure that the students will stop at a natural distance when beginning the conversation.
2. On the chalkboard, note as accurately as possible the distance between the two speakers with one line.
3. Half-way through their conversation, have the two students get as close as 30 centimeters and continue talking.
4. Measure the distance marked in Step 2 on the board.
5. Repeat the same process with a male/female combination.
6. Elicit the participants' feelings when the distance is minimized.
7. Ask the observers what they noticed in terms of changes in the participants' physical behavior.
8. Lead the class into a discussion of how various factors such as status, power, gender, intimacy, and different settings for communication influence the use of interpersonal distances for intercultural exploration. Use Hall's model, "American Cultural Interpersonal Distances for Various Categories of Interaction" (in Samovar & Porter, 1991, p. 218) as a basis for comparing and contrasting the patterns of the target culture with those of the learners' cultures.

Caveats and Options

1. This activity can be used to develop emotional as well as descriptive vocabulary about how the participants and the observers felt after the demonstration.
2. This task can also be used as group work in which students are asked to form a group of three (two of them to interact and one to measure distances of participants) and given various situations for interactions. The following are sample situations to act upon:
   - riding on an uncrowded train with people you do not know
   - talking to one's boss in his or her office
   - talking to a friend about something personal in the hallway
   - talking to a stranger who asks you for directions on a street
3. After the demonstrations, ask each group to report differences in the use of interpersonal distances to the class.

References and Further Reading

Samovar, L. A., & Porter, R. E. (1991). *Communication between cultures*. Belmont, CA: Wadsworth.

Contributor

Hiroyuki Umeno received an MA in TESOL at Temple University Japan, in Tokyo.

Body Language With an Accent

Levels
Intermediate +

Aims
Develop awareness of
cross-cultural issues
Develop awareness of
different nonverbal
communication styles
Realize the significance
of nonverbal
communication in
misunderstandings
Develop strategies to
prevent and recover
from miscommunication

Class Time
45 minutes

Preparation Time
10 minutes

Resources
Chalkboard, note cards

This activity helps students realize the significance of nonverbal communication by giving them an opportunity to analyze a misunderstanding from a safe distance and in a relaxed setting.

Procedure

1. Place students in small groups of three or four people (of mixed cultures preferably).
2. Write *communication* on the chalkboard. Below it, write *verbal* and *nonverbal*.
3. Ask students to define these terms in their groups.
4. Write their definitions on the chalkboard. Ask students for examples of each idea.
5. Add the prefix *mis-* before *communication*.
6. Ask a student to explain the new meaning of the word.
7. Write the new definition on the board.
8. Give each group one note card with an example of miscommunication caused by different nonverbal communication styles. Choose from the following or generate your own situations (see the Appendix for special notes to the teacher):
   - An American teacher in Japan has just finished a complicated lesson. Judging by his students' calm, blank facial expressions, he decides that his students understand everything, so he continues in the chapter. His students continue to be confused.
   - An English teacher in Vietnam wishes his students "Good luck!" by crossing his fingers. The students are embarrassed.
   - In an international business meeting, an American is sitting on one side of the table; an Arab and a Latin American are sitting

very close to the American. The American ends the meeting early and quickly leaves the room.

- A teacher is introduced to an elderly Indian. The teacher looks the Indian in the eye and says, "How do you do?" The Indian is insulted.
- An American is walking in another country and is shocked to see men holding hands with men and women with their arms around women.
- A newcomer to the United States is surprised at how friendly Americans are. She thinks that it is strange that they smile at people they don't know.

9. Have students in each group discuss what is happening in the situation. They should answer these questions:
   - What are some causes of the misunderstandings?
   - What could have been done to prevent such problems?
   - What can be done when a similar misunderstanding occurs?

10. Reconvene the class so that all students are in a big circle facing each other. Each group
    - reads its situation aloud
    - explains what could have been done to prevent the misunderstanding
    - predicts what can be done when a similar situation occurs

Caveats and Options

1. Ask more advanced students to perform these scenes aloud or to write their own scenes and perform them.
2. Rotate the cards so that each group works on two scenes.
3. Instead of using note cards, put all of the situations onto one handout.
4. Have students act as cultural experts of their country.
5. Create more stories and situations involving cultures represented in your classroom. It is important to have ESL and EFL situations and to have different people involved in the misunderstanding.
6. For homework before or after the lesson, have students write about specific nonverbal communication styles from their cultures or have them write about cross-cultural misunderstandings that they have experienced.

7. A discussion of stereotypes and generalizations may be necessary.
8. Be prepared to emphasize that culture is relative and that no style is inherently right or correct.

References and Further Reading

Levine, D. R., & Adelman, M. B. (1993). *Beyond language: Cross-cultural communication* (2nd ed.). Englewood Cliffs, NJ: Prentice Hall.

Appendix: Responses to Situations in Step 8

- Japanese people tend to limit their facial expressions in public situations such as a classroom.
- In Vietnam, crossing one's fingers is an insulting gesture that should be avoided.
- Americans tend to need more personal space than people from Arabic and Latin American cultures.
- It is disrespectful in India to make direct eye contact with a person older than oneself.
- Americans tend to limit their displays of affection among people of the same sex.
- A smile can have different meanings in different cultures.

Contributor

Sarah E. Upshaw recently completed her MS in applied linguistics and ESL at Georgia State University, in the United States, where she is currently teaching English for academic purposes.

Design Your Own Dream House

Levels
Intermediate +

Aims
Learn how the interior
of a U.S. home
compares with that of
homes in the students'
own countries
Learn vocabulary related
to home furnishings
Practice describing
homes by participating
in a group activity

Class Time
2–3 hours

Preparation Time
15 minutes

Resources
Magic markers or
crayons, flip chart paper
for each group
Tape or thumbtacks for
the flip chart, paper
Photocopies of diagram
of interior of a U.S.
home

This activity gives students the chance to learn about the layout of homes in the United States. Students will learn vocabulary for furniture and other objects typically found in U.S. houses by viewing a diagram of a home. In small groups, students will draw a group picture of their dream house and then share their picture with the rest of the class.

Procedure

1. Ask students to describe the homes in which they live in their own countries. Elicit the functions of all the rooms in the homes. Ask if people usually own their homes or rent them.
2. Distribute photocopies of a diagram of a U.S. home.
3. Ask students to describe what they see and to try to explain the purpose of each room. Elicit the names of particular pieces of furniture and the names of the rooms in the home.
4. Solicit and discuss similarities and differences between students' own homes and the U.S. home represented in the diagram.
5. Ask students what a *dream house* means. If no one knows, provide a definition (e.g., the ideal house a person would love to live in).
6. Divide class into groups of four to five students. Give markers and flip chart paper to each group.
7. Tell each group to design a dream house. Students must discuss what their house will look like and then draw a picture of it on the flip chart paper with the markers or crayons. They need to determine the following:
   - what rooms are in the house and what furniture goes in what room
   - what the exterior of the house looks like (e.g., the landscaping)
   - how many people live in the house and who they are
   - where in the world the house is located (it can be anywhere)

196

8. Tell each group to choose a spokesperson to explain their group's picture to the whole class.

9. When all groups have finished drawing, ask which group would like to go first to explain its picture. Attach the picture to the board or wall of the room so everyone can see it. Tell the class that after each spokesperson has talked, other members of the same group may add information. Then, students from other groups can ask questions to that group. Continue in the same manner until all groups have finished.

10. Ask the class if there are any common elements in the drawings from the groups. If yes, ask why that might be—what cultural aspects or values might be indicated as a result? Ask the students if they think those aspects or values are present in U.S. culture as well. Discuss why or why not.

Caveats and Options

1. One source for a good diagram of a U.S. home may be found in *Conversation in English: Points of Departure* (Dobson & Sedwick, 1981, p. 16). A useful list of vocabulary words pertaining to the home is given on page 17. Alternatively, teachers may draw their own diagrams and write their own vocabulary lists.

2. Pictures depicting various rooms in homes may be used instead of a diagram of a home. The teacher can divide the class into small groups and distribute one or two pictures to each group. Students can discuss what they see and then describe their pictures to the rest of the class.

References and Further Reading

Dobson, J. M., & Sedwick, F. (1981). *Conversation in English: Points of departure* (2nd ed.) Boston: Heinle & Heinle.

Gaston, J. (1984). *Cultural awareness teaching techniques*. Brattleboro, VT: Pro Lingua Associates.

Contributor

Susan L. Schwartz has taught ESL/EFL and U.S. culture in a variety of contexts in the United States and at universities in China and Indonesia.

As the World (Takes) Turns

Levels
Advanced; ESL and ESL teacher education students

Aims
Contribute to class discussion
Appreciate the longer wait time customary in other cultures
Have chance to speak and to listen to fellow classmates

Class Time
15 minutes

Preparation Time
10 minutes

Resources
One index card/student

This activity imposes an artificial structure on the taking of turns in a classroom discussion that results in an exploration of an important intercultural issue.

Procedure

1. Arrange students and self in a circle.
2. Inform students that during the class discussion, they will also learn how to take turns contributing to a discussion using different cultural rules.
3. Shuffle the turn-taking cards, hold them face down, and go around the circle, allowing each student to select a card.
4. Inform students of the rules for turn-taking in this activity:
   - The instructor asks the opening question for discussion.
   - It is then the responsibility of the student who drew Card 1 to speak.
   - No one else may speak while the Card 1 student has the floor.
   - When the Card 1 student has finished, the turn passes to Card 2 student.
   - Turn-taking proceeds until the student who drew the highest number for turn-taking has spoken.
   - The instructor then introduces another topic and the turn-taking procedure begins again.
   - The instructor allows 5 minutes at the end of the period to discuss the turn-taking activity itself within an intercultural context.

Caveats and Options

1. Offer a "Pass" option that allows a student to pass when his/her turn comes.

2. More effective than Option 1 is to allow an "I-need-more-time-to-think" option. This allows a student to temporarily pass his or her turn to the next person while at the same time understanding that the turn will return to her or him when the student with the highest number has spoken. The student whose turn it is decides how long to wait before exercising either this option or Option 1.

3. In addition to numbered cards, you may prepare a few "X" cards. These cards should amount to about 25% of the total number of students, and the numbered cards should be reduced by that percentage.

   Both the numbered and X-marked cards are shuffled together and, face down, can be selected by the students. Those selecting the "X" cards, however, do not have to wait their turn; instead they have the option of interrupting the turn-taking procedure whenever another student has finished. In other words, "X" card holders can jump into the conversation without waiting a turn.

4. After learning and using the turn-taking activity, the group itself can generate its own rules.

5. Have the students generate a similar, well-focused intercultural activity that can be incorporated into classroom meeting times.

6. While remarkably simple in conception, this turn-taking activity is powerful in exposing students to the feelings others have when their culture rule expectations are not adhered to. While using this activity, most U.S. students feel the frustration of waiting to speak, then gradually come to appreciate the longer wait times common in many international cultures and are able to translate this into their ESL teaching experience. On the other hand, this activity pressures international students to contribute, usually without enough time to prepare and with the discomfort of speaking in the presence of a teacher. They, too, come to appreciate rules of another culture and can begin to translate this into their teaching of EFL students bound for the Western world.

References and Further Reading

Anderson, G. G. (1992). *Multicultural sensitivity: An essential skill for the ESL/EFL teacher.* Unpublished master's thesis, School for International Training, Brattleboro, VT.

Mantle-Bromley, C. (1992). Preparing students for meaningful culture learning. *Foreign Language Annals, 25*, 117–127.

Contributor

Ruth Johnson is assistant professor in the Department of Linguistics at Southern Illinois University at Carbondale, in the United States.

How Do We Handle This?

Levels
Intermediate +

Aims
Develop empathy for
those with whom they
interact and/or counsel
Address cross-cultural
aspects of health and
illness issues
Gain an understanding
of the multifaceted
aspects of counseling:
cultural, cross-cultural,
spiritual, personal,
economic, emotional,
and medical

Class Time
45–60 minutes

Preparation Time
10–15 minutes

Resources
Envelope/group contain-
ing small pieces of
paper with each of the
roles printed on them
Copies of case study
and directions for every
student or every small
group

Of the many dimensions of an intercultural experience, health and illness often present some of the most sensitive and serious concerns. This activity offers an enjoyable, yet real way of looking at the cross-cultural dimensions of these important issues. Individual and cultural ethics often enter into the discussion quite naturally as do spiritual values. Students will have to look at their own values in life and see how they compare with those of their fellow students and the cultures they represent.

Procedure

1. Remind students of the importance of cross-cultural dimensions of their class work, and introduce the following case study involving a youth exchange program at the local middle school or high school:

Case Study

Your local middle/high school has been participating in a year-long cultural exchange program. There are only 2 weeks left in the program when 14-year-old Marcus becomes injured in a soccer game and is taken to the local hospital for what is believed to be a simple fracture of his right thigh. X-ray films and other medical tests at the hospital not only indicate the fractured leg, but pick up on a much more serious condition. All the other tests confirm the physician's conclusion that Marcus has osteosarcoma, cancer of the bone, in his right thigh.

---

2. Ask the class to consider how this situation should be dealt with and to consider all the parties involved: the youth, his family, his host family, and the hosting program.
3. Divide the class into groups of six or seven, depending on class size.

4. Have an envelope for each group, indicating the various roles students will assume; have each student select one slip of paper. Direct them as follows:

● You are to assume the following role as indicated by your slip of paper:

1. director of the cultural exchange program
2. host family of the youth involved
3. youth involved in the situation
4. physician who has made the diagnosis
5. & 6. parents of the youth involved in the accident
7. family physician/oncology specialist for the family in the youth's own country

● You should discuss the situation in your small groups as follows:

1. Physicians, youth and parent(s) discuss the situation at hand from their perspectives.
2. All other individuals discuss the issue from the perspectives of those hosting the exchange and how they think the situation should be handled.

● Groups: Share your insights and methods of handling the situation with the whole class, giving reasons for your decisions.

Caveats and Options

1. This activity can emphasize language use and/or cultural exploration in an adult leadership training program for teachers and others in charge of cross-cultural programs for youth. While stressing comparative and contrastive aspects of health issues, it leads to exploration of multiple dimensions of the intercultural experience. This activity is also useful for training teachers, counselors, and others dealing with students of ESL.

Contributor

Rebecca Banks was a psychological and educational consultant specializing in cross-cultural training/counseling and health counseling in Lakewood, Colorado, in the United States. She was also coeditor of Interspectives, the cross-cultural journal of CISV International in Newcastle, England.

D.I.C.E.: Many Sides to What We "See"*

Levels
Intermediate +

Aims
Learn to observe
behavior at the
descriptive,
nonjudgmental level
Develop awareness of
how words are laden
with judgments
Practice checking
interpretations of
observed behavior

Class Time
1–2 hours over several
sessions

Preparation Time
1 hour +

Resources
D.I.C.E. definitions on
newsprint
Index cards with
observations of other
cultures

This activity is a variation of the familiar "description, interpretation, evaluation" (D.I.E.) model for practicing nonjudgmental observation. Students will first practice turning their judgments (interpretations and evaluations) into descriptions. Then, "checking" is added, giving us D.I.C.E. By checking their interpretations, students get closer to understanding what is really going on and, therefore, may not get caught making hasty (and often negative) evaluations, a major barrier to communication.

Procedures

1. Data for this activity can be generated in one of the following ways depending on how much time you have to prepare and the risk level appropriate for the group:
   - Ask students to write two or three observations of behavior they have seen. These can be general or can be target-specific categories such as: in the classroom, at work, shopping, in a restaurant. (high risk)
   - Have individual students or small groups generate a list of 5–10 words describing U.S. Americans or other nationalities, or a subculture such as business people, professional athletes, and so on. (moderate risk)
   - Display a picture of a person alone or of people engaged in an activity. Have students write a description of what they see. (low risk)

---

* The C of D.I.C.E. comes from a workshop conducted by Stella Ting-Toomey, "Teaching Intercultural Communication," at the Summer Institute for Intercultural Communication, Portland, Oregon, July 1993.

2. Organize students into small groups of two to four each to work with the data generated in Step 1. Students should share their answers.

3. Bring students back to the large group. Post the explication of D.I.C.E., focusing on description for this part. Ask for comments or questions. (Students may point out that objectivity in description is very difficult.)

    ● description: what you objectively observe
    ● interpretation: how you explain the observed behavior
    ● checking: how you confirm your interpretation
    ● evaluation: how you judge the observed behavior

    Take a couple of examples from the small groups and decide which category they fall into—D, I, or E.

4. In small groups, have students decide if their data is D, I, or E, and, if I or E, change to D.

    For example: Americans are friendly. (I and E)
    D = Americans make contact with strangers easily (or more easily than in my culture)/smile a lot/use first names/initiate conversations with strangers.

5. Ask small groups to summarize this experience, that is, how easy/ difficult it is to get to description, at what level we usually operate, into which categories most words fall, and so on. Discuss in the large group. (The primary point is how most words are heavily laden with interpretation and/or evaluation.)

6. Ask students for examples in which their interpretation of someone's behavior was incorrect. After you have three to five examples, ask the students how they can check whether an interpretation is correct or not. Write up a list.

7. For homework have students

    ● write up an observation keeping it at the descriptive level
    ● write one or two interpretations of the observed behavior
    ● check their interpretation using one or two of the methods from the list
    ● report in the next class period

8. Finish with a discussion of the importance of checking interpretations and delaying evaluations.

Caveats and Options

1. Many words are both interpretations and evaluations—that is, they have a negative or positive meaning. For example, *hardworking* to describe Americans is an interpretation of their active behavior, and at the same time, is a positive value in U.S. culture.
2. As a variation, present a list of behaviors (descriptions) and have the students write five to six interpretations for each one. (This is similar to using critical incidents; see Brislin et al., 1986.)
3. Unless you know the group well and the students are comfortable with each other, use low-risk activities. Any data generated by the group carries with it less risk (of failure or loss of face) than individual responses.

References and Further Reading

Brislin, R., Cushner, K., Cherrie, C., & Yong, M. (1986). *Intercultural interactions: A practical guide.* Beverly Hills, CA: Sage. (Contains 100 critical incidents with 4 interpretations for each)

Fantini, A. E. (Ed.). (1984). *Cross-cultural orientation: A guide for leaders and educators.* Brattleboro, VT: The Experiment in International Living. Available from the SIT Bookstore, Brattleboro, VT. (Provides a list of adjectives that six nationalities ascribed to U.S. Americans; in Part II, p. 17, of the Student Guide)

Fieg, J., & Blair, J. (1989). *There is a difference: 17 intercultural perspectives* (2nd ed.). Washington, DC: Meridian House International. (Entire volume is quotes by other nationalities about U.S. Americans)

Storti, C. (1992). *The art of crossing cultures.* Yarmouth, ME: Intercultural Press. (Appendix 1 gives quotes about U.S. Americans)

Storti, C. (1994). *Cross-cultural dialogues: 74 brief encounters with cultural difference.* Yarmouth, ME: Intercultural Press. (Analyses of these miscommunications are rich in plausible interpretations)

Contributor

Carolyn Ryffel is an independent consultant specializing in intercultural communication, foreign language training (ESL, Spanish, German) and cross-cultural training.

Turn Off the Stereo(type)

Levels
Any

Aims
Explore assumptions
held about various
cultures and their
validity
Rethink commonly held
stereotypical
impressions

Class Time
1 hour

Preparation Time
10 minutes

Resources
None

Asking learners to identify stereotypes they hold about each other and themselves may help bring these myths into awareness. Discussion and comparison of widely held stereotypes may also highlight falsehoods and thus relieve their stereotypical impressions so that learners discover more about each other.

Procedure

1. Give students the Identifying Stereotypes handout (see Appendix), and ask them to fill it in.
2. Have them form small groups and compare their responses.
3. Have them use the handout to develop a questionnaire, the purpose of which is to ask people from the culture being stereotyped whether they believe the stereotype is a valid one.
4. Have the groups report their findings to the class.
5. Hold a discussion on the validity of stereotypes.

Caveats and Options

1. Interviewing people from various countries about positive and negative aspects of English-speaking people, of themselves, and of each other, could be one follow-up activity to reduce stereotypical impressions. Substitute other groups from those on the handout as necessary.

Appendix: Identifying Stereotypes

A. Americans (are)

always _____.

never _____.

sometimes _____.

like _____.

don't like _____.

B. The English (are)

always _____.

never _____.

sometimes _____.

like _____.

don't like _____.

C. Australians (are)

always _____.

never _____.

sometimes _____.

like _____.

don't like _____.

D. I (am)/we (are)

always _____.

never _____.

sometimes _____.

like _____.

don't like _____.

Contributor

Yoshiyuki Nakata received an MA in TESL from St. Michael's College. He currently is a full-time lecturer at Hinomoto Gakuen Junior College, in Japan.

All the Time in the World

Levels
Intermediate +

Aims
Realize that some
cultures view time very
differently from others
Observe how language
reflects the way we
view the world

Class Time
45 minutes–1½ hours

Preparation Time
30 minutes

Resources
Questionnaire on time
Handout on sayings in
English about time

Procedure

1. Group students and ask them to discuss the following questions:
   In your culture(s), how would people react if:
   - someone arrived
       early for work?
       exactly on time?
       20 minutes late?
   - a train arrived at the station
       earlier than scheduled?
       exactly on time?
       20 minutes late?
   - a guest arrived for dinner
       15 minutes earlier than invited?
       precisely at the time specified by the host?
       an hour later than the time of invitation?
2. Select different groups to report on the different sets of questions and then discuss the findings with the whole class.
3. Give each student the following list of expressions in English concerning time (adapted from Lakoff & Johnson, 1980):
   - Do you have any time to spare?
   - Thank you for giving me your time.
   - The plane lost time due to the strong prevailing winds.
   - There isn't enough time to do that now.
   - How did you spend your free time?
   - I need to put aside some time to catch up on my correspondence.
   - "Doctor, the patient is bleeding. We're running out of time."
   - Don't waste my time making excuses.

- Our new food processor will save you hours of preparation time.
- She's investing a lot of time in her new job at the bank.

4. Have students match the statements above with the following three metaphorical statements:
   - Time is money.
   - Time is a limited resource.
   - Time is a valuable commodity.
5. Ask students to discuss in their groups whether time is viewed in a similar way in their own culture(s).

Caveats and Options

1. The second part of this activity requires greater reflection and language ability. The two parts could be spread over two class sessions.
2. Students could also be invited to write down lists of expressions in their own language concerning time and invited to talk about how these reflect the way time is viewed in their own culture(s).
3. With more advanced classes, a follow-up discussion could be planned during which the teacher helps students to consider how common expressions reflect our way of thinking about certain concepts. For example:
   - Love is madness: She's *crazy* about the guy.
   - Love is war: She *fought off* his *advances.*
   - Love is magic: He was *bewitched* by her *charms.*

   Students could be asked to think of other examples that illustrate cultural values.

References and Further Reading

Lakoff, G., & Johnson, J. (1980). *Metaphors we live by.* Chicago: The University of Chicago Press.

Contributor

Dominic Cogan is a lecturer in English at Fukui Prefectural University, Japan. Previously he taught ESL/EFL at different levels in Ireland, Ghana, and Oman.

Rub Noses to Greet

Levels
Any

Aims
Practice introductions in
English
Develop curiosity about
other students
Develop empathy
toward cultural
differences when
meeting people

Class Time
1 hour

Preparation Time
5 minutes

Resources
Video examples of
culture-specific
introductions if available

Greetings and first impressions count in any culture. Knowing how to play the role can help students develop cultural sensitivity and increase their chances of being accepted.

Procedure

1. Introduce the activity by talking about and demonstrating how people meet and greet in different cultures. Give a variety of examples, such as:
   - how the Maoris in New Zealand traditionally rub noses
   - how the Japanese bow at different degrees depending on the people they meet
   - how Koreans kowtow to greet in the house by kneeling and lowering their heads
   - and how Thai people put their palms together and place them at different heights in front of their face depending on the assumed importance of the person
   Videotaped examples enhance this step.
2. Encourage students to talk about experiences and feelings when they met different people of the same/different cultural background.
3. Describe and demonstrate how to greet in English, including how to shake hands while mentioning the meanings associated with weak/strong handshakes. Other extralinguistic factors such as distance and eye contact are worth mentioning.
4. Practice greetings in pairs or groups.
5. Have students write the dialogues.

Caveats and Options

1. Students can be asked to write a comparison and contrast paper on the cultural differences in greetings between people of their own culture and the target language culture.
2. Younger students may enjoy being given an English name to help them to step into the shoes of the culture—they enjoy the opportunity to use a foreign name for a role in a foreign greeting setting.

References and Further Reading

Levine, D., Baxter, J., & McNulty, P. (1987). *The culture puzzle.* Englewood Cliffs, NJ: Prentice Hall.

Contributors

Elizabeth Lange and Jong-oe Park have taught students of many different cultural and language backgrounds. Lange is presently teaching college students in Japan. Park has taught English to college students and adults in South Korea and Japan.

A Selective and Annotated Bibliography of Works on Language and Culture

*Compiled by
Alvino E. Fantini and
Carolyn Ryffel*

Offering works on the topic of teaching language and culture, this bibliography is categorized into six areas to help ESOL teachers find effective materials for incorporating culture and intercultural dimensions into the language classroom:

1. Intercultural Theory and Models
2. Intercultural Communicative Competence
3. Cultural Differences Affecting Teaching-Learning
4. Integrating Culture Into the Language Classroom
5. Cross-Cultural Activities and Their Effective Use
6. Specific Cultures and Countries

1. Intercultural Theory and Models

Agar, M. (1994). *Language shock: Understanding the culture of conversation*. New York: William Morrow. A book about cultural differences and how these are unconsciously reflected through everyday language use.

American Council on the Teaching of Foreign Languages. (1995). *National standards in foreign language education*. Yonkers, NY: Author. Developed by a Foreign Language Standards Committee charged with the task of developing national standards for foreign languages in the United States for students from kindergarten through Grade 12. The document sets out five major goal areas for foreign language education that integrate language, culture, and intercultural perspectives.

Bennett, M. (1993). A developmental approach to training for intercultural sensitivity. In M. Paige (Ed.), *Education for the intercultural experience* (pp. 21–77). Yarmouth, ME: Intercultural Press. Provides a theoretical framework for understanding student and teacher reaction to difference. The continuum spans the ethnocentric stages of denial, defense, and minimization, and the ethnorelative stages of acceptance, adaptation, and adoption/integration. Provides examples of what people say and do at each stage when confronted with difference.

Chilton Pearce, J. (1971). *The crack in the cosmic egg: Challenging constructs of mind and reality*. New York: Washington Square Press. A provocative essay on the relation of mind and reality—the mirroring of thinking and experience. The *cosmic egg* the author describes as the "sum total of our notions of what the world is, notions which define what reality can be for us." The crack, then, is a mode of thinking through which imagination can escape the mundane shell and create a new cosmic egg. A fascinating exploration of language, culture, and world view of interest to the language teacher.

Classen, C. (1993). *Worlds of sense: Exploring the senses in history and across cultures*. New York: Routledge. Examines the different sensory world views of various cultures, such as societies that emphasize olfaction or touch over visual sensing, providing an unusual and little-known perspective on an important dimension of intercultural communication.

Eastman, C. M. (1990). *Aspects of language and culture* (2nd ed.) Novato, CA: Chandler & Sharp. The relevant chapter, "Language and Culture," is divided into two sections: "World View" (pp. 103–127) and "Language, Thought and Reality" (pp. 127–140). The first section summarizes works of Sapir, Whorf, and Fishman, along with work on methodologies of cognitive anthropology. The second part links the previous section to the study of pragmatics, semiotics, and social identity. Eastman poses questions about world view and language raised by generative linguistics, finding theories of universal grammar compatible with a weak version of the Whorfian hypothesis.

Fantini, A. E. (1992). Exploring language, culture and world view. *Interspectives: A Journal on Transcultural and Peace Education, 2,* 13–16. Explores connections between language, culture, and world view from an intercultural perspective. It underscores the need to develop skills in a second language as a transformative process, effecting a change in world view. Fantini extends the notion of language as communicative competence to include intercultural communication, advocating "intercultural communicative competence" as a means of improving interpersonal and cross-cultural effectiveness.

Fantini, A. E. (Ed.). (1995). Special issue on Language, Culture and World View. *International Journal of Intercultural Relations, 19*(2). A collection of works by researchers representing a wide variety of perspectives from different language and culture backgrounds who are attempting to make the connections between language and culture that together represent one's world view. The introductory article by Fantini is of particular interest to language teachers and presents several models for linking language and culture that have direct implications for language education.

Goodman, N. (1994). Intercultural education at the university level: Teacher-student interaction. In R. Brislin & T. Yoshida (Eds.), *Improving intercultural interactions: Modules for cross-cultural training programs* (pp. 129–147). Thousand Oaks, CA: Sage. Presents a training plan for having teachers explore their assumptions and beliefs about the teaching situation. It includes a Self-Assessment Exercise for Instructional Styles based on Hofstede's (1991) dimensions of collectivism/individualism and power distance.

Gudykunst, W., & Kim, Y. (1992). *Communicating with strangers: An approach to intercultural communication* (2nd ed.). New York: McGraw-Hill. Entire volume offers a solid introduction to the field of intercultural communication. Of special interest to language teachers are the chapters on verbal behavior, nonverbal behavior, and effectiveness in communicating with strangers. The chapter covering cultural influences on the communication process has an especially good discussion of individualism-collectivism.

Hall, E. T. (1959, 1981). *The silent language*; (1966, 1982) *The hidden dimension*; (1976, 1981) *Beyond culture*; and (1983) *The dance of life*. All published by Anchor/Doubleday and available as a set through Yarmouth, ME: Intercultural Press. The classics of the intercultural field in which Hall looks at cultural differences and how they affect human relations.

Hofstede, G. (1991). *Cultures and organizations: Software of the mind*. London: McGraw-Hill. Of the two books by Hofstede covering his theory of four dimensions of national cultural differences, this one is the more manageable for the uninitiated and expands the theory further to include a fifth dimension—Confucian Dynamism. Includes a section on implications for education.

Nelson, G. L. (in press). *Intercultural communication or "culture" courses in graduate TESOL programs.* A survey of intercultural communication courses offered in TESOL programs, with notes on their design, content, processes, and materials.

Paige, M., & Martin, J. (1996). Ethics in intercultural training. In D. Landis & R. Bhagat (Eds.), *Handbook of intercultural training* (2nd ed., pp. 35–60). Thousand Oaks, CA: Sage. Discusses the ethics of culture teaching and learning, emphasizing the welfare of the learner, plus a section on the ethical intercultural trainer that reviews goals and objectives, types of activities, risk level, and social-psychological learning environments, to name a few.

Purves, A. C. (Ed.). (1988). *Writing across languages and cultures: Issues in contrastive rhetoric.* Newbury Park, CA: Sage. Specifically addresses how cultural differences affect writing by foreign students in educational settings. Offers four theoretical chapters, including one by Kaplan, and seven chapters contrasting specific cultures or culture groups. Extremely important for anyone teaching composition.

Reid, J. M. (1995/1996, December/January). Let's put the "T" back in TESOL/TEFL. *TESOL Matters,* p. 3. Reviews the design and content of teacher preparation programs in TESL/TEFL. Among the findings is the startling statistic that only about one third of programs even offer a course in culture. Points to the need for increased attention to the culture and intellectual dimension of language teaching.

Samovar, L. A., & Porter, R. E. (1991). *Communication between cultures.* Belmont, CA: Wadsworth. Designed to help develop an appreciation and understanding of different cultures, plus the practical skills needed to communicate with people from cultures other than your own.

Samovar, L. A., & Porter, R. E. (1991). *Intercultural communication: A reader* (6th ed.) Belmont: CA: Wadsworth. Contains 19 essays about cultures, both within the United States and globally, providing both theoretical and immediately usable knowledge about intercultural communication processes. Aids understanding of barriers to effective communication, a topic of interest to ESOL teachers.

TESOL. (1996). *Promising futures: ESL standards for pre-K–12 students.* TESOL Professional Papers #1. Alexandria, VA: Author. A guide for ESL and bilingual specialists, classroom teachers, and other educational professionals involved in the education of pre-K–12 ESOL students in the United States. The document establishes three important goals for ESL that include under Goal 3 "the ability to use English in socially and culturally appropriate ways," therein linking language learning with culture and intercultural learning.

Tickoo, M. L. (1995). *Language and culture in multilingual societies: Viewpoints and visions.* Anthology Series 36. Singapore: SEAMEO Regional Language Centre/Sherson Publishing House. Entire volume is a compilation of articles by 17 contributors from around the world addressing the topic of language and culture from various points of view, including research, training, and education.

Victor, D. (1992). *International business communication.* New York: HarperCollins. Although focused on international business applications, this book offers excellent explanations of high/low context and is especially strong in describing *face.*

2. Intercultural Communicative Competence

Biber, D., & Finegan, E. (Eds.). (1994). *Sociolinguistic perspectives on register.* New York: Oxford University Press. A collection of perspectives on language varieties defined according to their contexts of use, variously called *registers, sublanguages,* or *genres.* Registers from languages around the globe are examined. The importance of these central linguistic phenomena to understanding connections between languages and their cultures is underscored and linked to the development of intercultural competence.

Brown, H. D. (1991). *Breaking the language barrier.* Yarmouth, ME: Intercultural Press. Explores critical elements of the language learning process that include the development of self-confidence, the discovery of one's individual learning style, and several other sociocultural aspects, such as the role of identity in language learning, motivation, and the importance of learning to make and tolerate mistakes. The work acknowledges intercultural effects on second language development.

Fantini, A. E. (1985). *Language acquisition of a bilingual child: A sociolinguistic perspective*. Brattleboro, VT: Bookstore, School for International Training. An analysis of language acquisition based on longitudinal observation of a child, bilingual in Spanish and English, from birth to age 10. A background section reviews literature on bilingualism and trends in sociolinguistics, while the main section explores the effect of socialization on developing bilingualism, particularly with regard to attitudes and behaviors, style shifting and code switching, and transfer across languages. The work provides a perspective of early stages leading to the development of intercultural competence.

Fantini, A. E. (1994). Developing intercultural communicative competence. *TESOL-Spain Quarterly Newsletter*, pp. 7–13. *Intercultural competence* is defined and proposed as an appropriate goal for many ESOL courses. The author cites three challenges for teachers, teacher education, and institutions.

Fantini, A. E. (1995). An expanded goal for language education: Developing intercultural communicative competence. In M. L. Tickoo (Ed.), *Language and culture in multilingual societies: Viewpoints and visions* (pp. 37–53). Anthology Series 36. Singapore: SEAMEO Regional Language Centre/Sherson Publishing House. Proposes intercultural competence as the goal for language instruction, providing a framework for developing such competence in the language classroom.

Kealey, D. J. (1990). *Cross-cultural effectiveness*. Hull, Canada: Canadian International Development Agency. A unique research project that attempts to explain and predict cross-cultural adjustment and effectiveness. Results of the study support the view that both knowledge of the local culture and participation in that culture are associated with overseas effectiveness. The study attempts to address issues about traits and other qualities leading to intercultural competence.

Krasnick, H. (1985). Intercultural competence in ESL for adults. *JALT Journal, 7*, 15–41.

Lustig, M. W., & Koester, J. (1993). *Intercultural competence: Interpersonal communication across cultures*. New York: HarperCollins. A useful text for teaching about intercultural competence with many implications and suggestions relevant to language teaching. Of special relevance are Chapters 7 and 8, which deal with both verbal and nonverbal competence.

Martin, J. (Ed.). (1989). Special Issue on Intercultural Communicative Competence. *International Journal of Intercultural Relations, 13*(3). An excellent collection of articles by various researchers attempting to define the notion of *intercultural communicative competence.*

Wiseman, R. L., & Koester, J. (Eds.). (1993). *Intercultural communication competency.* Newbury Park, CA: Sage. Gathers current research, theories, and methods from leading scholars in the field on the topic of intercultural communication competence.

3. Cultural Differences Affecting Teaching-Learning

Althen, G. (Ed.). (1994). *Learning across cultures* (2nd ed.). Washington, DC: NAFSA: Association of International Educators. (Available through Intercultural Press.) Focuses on international educational exchange; intercultural communication theory and practice is presented in that context. The chapters on cultural adjustment, classroom management, and cultural differences on the campus are especially noteworthy.

Brislin, R., Cushner, K., Cherrie, C., & Yong, M. (1986). *Intercultural interactions.* Beverly Hills, CA: Sage. Offers 100 "critical incidents" illustrating common experiences in interacting with people from other cultures. Each short incident is followed by four possible explanations; at the end of each section the choices are analyzed. One of the eight sections covers education and schooling.

Byrd, P. (Ed.). (1986). *Teaching across cultures in the university ESL program.* Washington, DC: NAFSA. Chapters by Furey and Fitch in "Part I: Background Discussions" are especially rich in material on how to look at cross-cultural differences in the assumptions teachers and students have about their roles, education, learning, and the classroom.

Hofstede, G. (1986). Cultural differences in teaching and learning. *International Journal of Intercultural Relations, 10,* 301–320. Relates Hofstede's model of four dimensions (4-D) of cultural differences to the dynamics of culturally mixed teacher/student pairs. Includes a good summary of the 4-D model and hypothetical descriptors for the extremes of each dimension in the cross-cultural learning situation.

Murray, D. (Ed.). (1992). *Diversity as resource: Redefining cultural literacy*. Alexandria, VA: TESOL. Written primarily for ESL and content-area teachers in the United States. The book's first three chapters expand definitions of both literacy and culture to acknowledge the vast range of contexts of language use. Then each of six chapters deals with a specific culture, that culture's view of literacy and how that affects their experience in the U.S. educational system.

Nelson, G. (1995). Cultural differences in learning styles. In J. Reid (Ed.), *Learning styles in the ESL/EFL classroom* (pp. 3–18). Boston: Heinle & Heinle. First determines that cultures, not just individuals, can have learning styles, and then analyzes in depth the learning styles of China and Japan. Especially useful is the section on implications detailing specific strategies teachers can use to address these cultural differences in the classroom.

Nemetz Robinson, G. L. (1988). *Crosscultural understanding*. Englewood Cliffs, NJ: Prentice Hall. Examines the teacher, the learner, the text and the curriculum as interrelated components of the classroom, all affected by values, perceptions, experiences, questions of identity, and so on. The book provides a good resource for interpreting and reflecting on classroom experiences. It reviews definitions of culture, the effect of culture on perception, cultural roles, ethnography, and multiculturalism as an aspect of ESOL.

Scarcella, R. (1990). *Teaching language minority students in the multicultural classroom*. Englewood Cliffs, NJ: Prentice Hall Regents. Although written for content-area teachers with language minority students, this volume incorporates very complete discussions of cultural differences that affect classroom behavior and responses.

Schmidt, R. W. (1983). Interaction, acculturation, and the acquisition of communicative competence. In N. Wolfson & E. Judd (Eds.), *Sociolinguistics and language acquisition* (pp. 137–174). Rowley, MA: Newbury House. A case study of the second language acquisition of an adult learner that goes beyond exploration of language in terms of forms, structures, and roles to an investigation of other components, with special concern for interactional and social aspects of language ability that form part of communicative competence.

Schumann, J. H. (1978). The acculturation model for second language acquisition. In R. Gingras (Ed.), *Second language acquisition and foreign language teaching.* Arlington, VA: Center for Applied Linguistics. An important work that explores how intercultural entry affects and influences the development of second language ability.

Schumann, J. H. (1976, June). Social distance as a factor in second language acquisition. *Language Learning, 26,* pp. 135-143. An examination of societal factors that inhibit or promote social distance and, therefore, language learning: dominance, group preservation, enclosure, cohesiveness, congruence, negative attitudes, and more. In essence, a review of cultural factors that may influence students' receptiveness of a foreign language, distinguishing between psychological distance (a person's attitude) and social distance (the values and patterns of a cultural group).

Stauble, A. E. (1980). Acculturation and second language acquisition. In R. C. Scarcella & S. D. Krashen (Eds.), *Research in second language acquisition* (pp. 43-50). Rowley, MA: Newbury House. An attempt to determine what factors are involved in influencing success in the second language learning process, with special focus on the effects of acculturative influences—such as social and psychological distance—that either promote or hinder the extent to which the second language learner will learn the target language.

Ting-Toomey, S., & Korzenny, F. (1989). *Language, communication, and culture: Current directions.* Newbury Park, CA: Sage. A collection of works representing varied disciplines on current developments in areas such as language acquisition within a cultural context and cognition; relationship between language and cross-cultural communication; and foreign/second language usage in intergroup communication contexts.

Valdes, J. M. (Ed.). (1986). *Culture bound: Bridging the cultural gap in language teaching.* New York: Cambridge University Press. A collection of articles dealing with the various skills and knowledge foreign language teachers need in order to assist their students in adjusting to living in another culture and to using the culture to promote language learning. Part 2 specifically addresses cultural differences that affect students in the classroom.

Wurzel, J., & Fischman, N. (1993). *A different place: The intercultural classroom.* [Video]. Newtonville, MA: Intercultural Resource Corporation. (Available through Intercultural Press.) This excellent video simulates a university classroom with both U.S. and international students. It highlights the behavior and reactions of the U.S. professor and the students, followed by individuals discussing how they felt. The instructional guide analyzes the cultural differences affecting the classroom behavior and details lesson plans. Appropriate for both faculty and students.

4. Integrating Culture Into the Language Classroom

American Council on the Teaching of Foreign Languages. (1996). *Standards for foreign language learning: Preparation for the 21st century*. Lawrence, KS: Allen Press/Author. A final report prepared by a national Foreign Languages Task Force of a 3-year project attempting to define standards for foreign language education in the United States. The standards were piloted with various schools throughout the country and were issued at the November 1995 national convention of the American Council on the Teaching of Foreign Languages.

Byram, M., & Morgan, C. (1994). *Teaching and learning language and culture*. Clevedon, England: Multilingual Matters. Cites several complex and integrated dimensions of foreign language learning, including acquisition of grammatical competence, change in attitudes, learning information about another country and people, and reflecting upon one's own culture and cultural identity. A major part of the book consists of case studies in language and culture teaching as well as the assessment of cultural learning.

Damen, L. (1987). *Culture learning: The fifth dimension in the language classroom*. Reading, MA: Addison Wesley. Perhaps the most comprehensive single resource on how to successfully integrate culture into the language classroom. Organized as a text with questions and exercises at the end of each chapter, it guides the teacher systematically in acquiring the knowledge and skills needed for successful integration. The two parts are, in fact, each equivalent to a single book. "Part 1: Theory, Research, and Practice in the Fields of Intercultural Communication and Second Language Learning/Teaching" reviews and synthesizes different theories of intercultural communication and language pedagogy. "Part 2: Practicum: Theory into Practice" applies the theory to the work of the language teacher.

Fantini, A. (1993). Focus on process: An examination of the learning and teaching of intercultural communicative competence. In T. Gochenour (Ed.), *Beyond experience: The experiential approach to cross-cultural education*. (rev. ed.; pp. 45–54). Yarmouth, ME: Intercultural Press. To respond effectively to the many different needs of the language learning situation, the author advocates that teachers work from a broad base of teaching methods, avoiding the trap of embracing one method to the exclusion of others. A seven-step process approach provides a framework for designing both curricula and lesson plans that ensure that the focus is on the development of intercultural communicative competence.

Fantini, A., & Dant, W. (1993). Language and intercultural orientation: A process approach. In T. Gochenour (Ed.), *Beyond experience: The experiential approach to cross-cultural education* (rev. ed., pp. 79–96). Yarmouth, ME: Intercultural Press. Building on Chapter 5 of the same volume, the seven stages of the process approach and corresponding teaching techniques are listed. A wide range of classroom activities for Stages 4 (Transposition) and 5 (Sociolinguistic Exploration) are then detailed.

Flewelling, J. L. (1994). The teaching of culture: Guidelines from the National Core French Study of Canada. *Foreign Language Annals, 27,* 133–142. A theoretical look at how and why culture should be taught in language programs with examples of cultural topics and practical activities to help integrate these topics into language teaching programs. A list of Canadian sources for cultural information is provided in the Appendix.

Hudson, T., Detmer, E., & Brown, J. D. (1992). *A framework for testing cross-cultural pragmatics*. Manoa: University of Hawaii. A technical report that presents a framework for developing methods to assess cross-cultural pragmatic ability. Although based on Japanese and U.S. contrasts, the framework is a generic approach that can be applied to other contrasts as well.

Kramsch, C. J. (1989). *New directions in the teaching of language and culture*. NFLC Occasional Papers. Washington, DC: National Foreign Language Center, Johns Hopkins University. A valuable review of current issues in the teaching of language and culture. This work traces traditional approaches, the current development of educational guidelines, objectives, political implications, and efforts to link the teaching of language and culture in the United States.

Kramsch, C. J. (1993). *Context and culture in language teaching*. Oxford: Oxford University Press. Emphasizes culture learning as integral to language learning, not an add-on skill, with cultural context as the core. Language proficiency is promoted by cultural awareness, which is itself promoted by language proficiency. Provides a theoretical framework with examples of practical applications for the classroom.

Levine, D. R. (1987). *Beyond language: Intercultural communication for English as a second language*. New York: Prentice Hall. An advanced culture reader that introduces ESOL students to the art of objective cultural observation and learning. Students look at the complexities of culture through readings and discussions. Helpful culture notes are included throughout.

Martin, J. N. (1986). Special Issue on Theories and Methods in Cross-Cultural Orientation *International Journal of Intercultural Relations, 10*(2). A collection of theories and methods common within the field of intercultural communication that have direct application to integrating culture and intercultural dimensions in the language classroom.

Mestenhauser, J. A., et al. (1988). *Culture, learning, and the disciplines*. Washington, DC: National Association for Foreign Student Affairs. A collection of works by various authors addressing both theory and practice in cross-cultural orientation.

Seelye, H. N. (1993). *Teaching culture: Strategies for intercultural communication* (3rd ed.). Lincolnwood, IL: National Textbook Co. The title spells out the essence of this work—how to teach culture. Addressing language educators in particular, the author provides a wealth of examples and "seven goals of cultural instruction" as a useful guide for the teaching of culture in the language classroom.

Special Edition on The Teaching of Culture. (1996). *Foreign Language Annals, 29*(1). Compiles articles by various individuals from varied contexts who address the importance and need to include the teaching of culture in language education.

Zander, V. V. (1993). *Face to face: Communication, culture and collaboration* (2nd ed.). Boston: Heinle & Heinle. Devoted to helping students learn English through cross-cultural exploration, the text enables students to interact in English by engaging in interview situations and conducting field-based research on U.S. culture.

5. Cross-Cultural Activities and Their Effective Use

Brislin, R., & Yoshida, T. (1994). *Intercultural communications training: An introduction*. Thousand Oaks, CA: Sage. A comprehensive guidebook providing an organizational framework for planning and establishing intercultural communication training programs. Includes assessing needs, establishing goals, and building positive attitudes.

Cushner, K., & Brislin, R. (1995). *Intercultural interactions: A practical guide* (2nd ed.). Beverly Hills, CA: Sage.

Damen, L. (1987). *Culture learning: The fifth dimension in the language classroom*. Reading, MA: Addison Wesley. "Part 2: Practicum: Theory Into Practice" applies the theory of Part 1 to developing class activities and lessons that will enhance culture learning.

Drum, J., Hughes, S., & Otero, G. (1994). *Global winners: 74 learning activities for inside and outside the classroom*. Yarmouth, ME: Intercultural Press. A rich resource book of 74 exercises, role plays, simulations, and other activities for use inside and outside of the classroom. The work focuses on K–12 students, expanding awareness of global and intercultural issues.

Fantini, A. (Ed.). (1984). *Cross-cultural orientation: A guide for leaders and educators*. Brattleboro, VT: The Experiment in International Living. (Available from the Bookstore, School for International Training, Brattleboro, VT 05302 USA.) Although this guide is primarily oriented toward student exchange groups, many of the activities for cross-cultural orientation can be easily adapted to the language classroom.

Fowler, S., & Mumford, M. (Eds.). (1995). *Intercultural sourcebook: Cross-cultural training methods* (vol. 1, 2nd ed.). Yarmouth, ME: Intercultural Press. This first volume contains the most up-to-date information on the background and use of specific methods used in cross-cultural training. Six of the eight sections dedicate three chapters each to specific training methods (role plays, culture contrast, simulation games, critical incidents, culture assimilators, and case studies). The value to the foreign language teacher is the instructions for effectively using each method—information often lacking in ESL/EFL materials.

Gaston, J. (1984). *Cultural awareness teaching techniques*. Brattleboro, VT: Pro Lingua Associates. An excellent resource on two levels: The 20 exercises themselves are designed to take the students through four stages in developing skills in cultural awareness and in intercultural adjustment. "Suggestions to the Teacher" sections address the issues in using these activities with students from a variety of cultures.

Gochenour, T. (Ed.). (1993). *Beyond experience: The experiential approach to cross-cultural education* (rev. ed.). Yarmouth, ME: Intercultural Press. A collection of articles by various contributors, divided into three sections (Ideas, Activities, and Assessment) providing: a conceptual framework for experiential cross-cultural education; a collection of essays on practical applications of these ideas along with specific exercises, simulations, and other activities; and a guide to assessing the educational impact of the experience. Many of these activities can be adapted for use in the language classroom.

Hess, J. D. (1994). *The whole world guide to culture learning*. Yarmouth, ME: Intercultural Press. Written for students preparing to go abroad, it is rich with background information on the entire range of intercultural topics. Each chapter begins with an informational introduction and follows with activities for culture learning. Good source of many experiences that the teacher could plan an activity around.

Kohls, R. (1984). *Survival kit for overseas living: For Americans planning to live and work abroad* (2nd ed.). Yarmouth, ME: Intercultural Press. A classic in the intercultural field. Although written for Americans going abroad, it can be useful to language teachers for several reasons: concise discussions of main issues in intercultural communication, exercises for Americans to develop self-awareness, and ideas for classroom activities.

Kohls, R., & Knight, J. M. (1994). *Developing intercultural awareness: A cross-cultural training handbook* (2nd ed.). Yarmouth, ME: Intercultural Press. Presents designs for 1- and 2-day workshops using the resources the rest of the book comprises. Any teacher using this as a source of activities must keep in mind that they are designed for U.S. Americans or possibly with U.S. Americans mixed with other nationalities; these activities are not designed for groups of only foreigners and, therefore, would need to be adapted.

Krasnick, H. (1988). Dimensions of cultural competence: Implications for the ESL curriculum. *TESL Reporter, 21*(3), 49-55.

Landis, D., & Bhagat, R. S. (Eds.). (1996). *Handbook of intercultural training* (2nd ed.). Thousand Oaks, CA: Sage. A collection of articles by various authors that analyzes regions of the world where intercultural issues of the 20th century have heightened in importance—including Central and South America, Europe, China, Eastern Europe, Russia, and Israel. Other sections of the book examine theoretical and methodological issues inherent in intercultural interactions and training and the contexts in which training takes place.

Pusch, M. (Ed.). (1979). *Multicultural education: A cross-cultural training approach.* Yarmouth, ME: Intercultural Press. The first part of the book provides a very concise explanation of the fields of intercultural communication and multicultural education. The last part contains cross-cultural training activities that can be adapted for ESOL use.

Seelye, H. N. (1993). *Teaching culture: Strategies for intercultural communication* (3rd ed.). Lincolnwood, IL: National Textbook Co.

Seelye, H. N. (1995). *Experiential activities for intercultural learning* (Vol. 1). Yarmouth, ME: Intercultural Press. This collection of 32 activities includes some that specifically target educational contexts. Of special relevance is Ramsey's introductory essay on factors to consider in choosing methodologies.

Storti, C. (1994). *Cross-cultural dialogues: 74 brief encounters with cultural difference.* Yarmouth, ME: Intercultural Press. Using short dialogues four to eight lines long, Storti demonstrates the degree to which culture, not language, can be the source of misunderstandings. The dialogues are organized in three sections: social, workplace, and business, and the sections are followed by a cultural analysis of each dialogue. Written for U.S. Americans interacting with someone from another culture (10 nationalities/regions are covered), these can nevertheless be used in the ESOL classroom for learning ways in which cultures differ and how that affects language use. Storti concludes with a useful chapter on how to write your own dialogues.

Summerfield, E. (1993). *Crossing cultures through film.* Yarmouth, ME: Intercultural Press. A rich resource that analyzes more than 70 films for enhancing cross-cultural learning. The films chosen deal with intercultural issues of nationality, race, and ethnicity only. Includes chapters on finding films and using them effectively, and then chapters grouping films according to cross-cultural objectives. Summerfield thoroughly discusses each film, includes a separate Tips for Use, and finishes each chapter listing related films.

Tomalin, B., & Stempleski, S. (1993). *Cultural awareness*. New York: Oxford University Press. As the title suggests, the more than 70 activities are intended to increase cross-cultural awareness specifically emphasizing the improvement of observation skills, confronting stereotypes, and ultimately developing tolerance while at the same time promoting language learning. The activities focusing on contrasts between US American/British culture and the students' culture(s) are structured to include the aim, material, level, time, step-by-step preparation, in-class use, and variations.

6. Specific Cultures and Countries

Brick, J. (1991). *China: A handbook in intercultural communication*. Sydney, Australia: Macquarie University. (Available through Alta.) This book, written for Australian English teachers, provides historical, cultural, and political information about China and links this information to the values, beliefs, and behavior of that culture. Included are activities for integrating cultural elements into the language class. Excellent explanations and examples illustrate the culture-language connection.

David M. Kennedy Center for International Studies. *Culturgram*. (Updated frequently). Provo, UT: Brigham Young University. The succinct and up-to-date fact sheets provide ready access to basic information about a multitude of cultures and countries, of use to the ESOL teacher.

Fantini, A. E., & Fantini, B. C. (1994). *Living in Mexico*; Fantini, A. E., & Enríquez, C. A. (1993). *Living in Spain*; (1996). *Living in Italy*. Brattleboro, VT: Pro Lingua. This series focuses on specific cultures and countries and includes others, in addition to those listed above. Each work in the series contains four parts: Part I: First Steps (about practical matters of getting around, e.g., money, food, restaurants). Part II: Customs and Values (provides information about e.g., greetings, titles, friendship, personal space). Part III: Country Facts (gives information about e.g., history, people, land, climate). Part IV: The Language (provides a brief summary of the language, its history and background, pronunciation, basic grammar, and useful expressions). A bibliography is also included. A useful source for finding quick and up-to-date information about specific cultures and countries.

Gannon, J., et al. (1994). *Understanding global cultures: Metaphorical journeys through 17 countries*. Thousand Oaks, CA: Sage. Using cultural metaphors as a device for enhancing understanding, Gannon analyzes the dominant national character of 17 countries. Examples of his metaphors include the Italian opera, French wine, American football, the dance of Shiva, and the Japanese garden. Informative and useful for the ESOL teacher.

Highwater, J. (1981). *The primal mind: Vision and reality in Indian America*. New York: Meridian. An exploration of the often misunderstood world of Native Americans, contrasting the ideas and intellectual aims of Western culture with the lifestyles, attitudes, and world views of North American tribal peoples and other primal peoples of the world. Examples of language expression of Native Americans are provided throughout, reinforcing connections between language and world view.

Hijirida, K., & Yoshikawa, M. (1987). *Japanese language and culture for business and travel: A text for students and travel industry managers.* Honolulu: University of Hawaii Press. This text for learning the Japanese language is filled with cultural explanations of the deepest assumptions underlying Japanese culture and its language. Each chapter begins with a Japanese lesson followed by sections called Culture Orientation, Japanese Mode of Communication, and Language and Culture.

Koyama, T. (1992). *Japan: A handbook in intercultural communication.* Sydney, Australia: Macquarie University. (Available through Alta). This book, written for Australian English teachers, provides historical, cultural, and political information about China and links this information to the values, beliefs and behavior of those cultures. Included are activities for integrating cultural elements into the language class. Excellent explanations and examples illustrating the culture-language connection.

Lanier, A. R. (1988). *Living in the U.S.A.* (4th ed.). Yarmouth, ME: Intercultural Press. A survey of what U.S. Americans are like and how they conduct their lives. A guide and compendium of customs, courtesies, and caveats giving practical advice for sojourners in the United States.

Sakamoto, N., & Naotsuka, R. (1982). *Polite fictions: Why Japanese and Americans seem rude to each other*. Tokyo, Japan: Kinseido. (Can also be purchased through Nancy Sakamoto, 1936 Citron St., Honolulu, HI 96826 USA.) Written as an EFL text for Japanese students with summaries in Japanese at the end of each chapter, this very entertaining volume offers a completely nonjudgmental view of what causes the clashes in interactions between U.S. Americans and Japanese—the conflicting polite fictions of each culture.

Stewart, E., & Bennett, M. (1991). *American cultural patterns: A cross-cultural perspective* (rev. ed.). Yarmouth, ME: Intercultural Press. A classic in explaining the assumptions, values, and beliefs that are the foundation of U.S. American behavior.

Suzuki, T. (1978, 1984). *Words in context: A Japanese perspective on language and culture* (A. Miura, Trans.). Tokyo: Kodansha International. Contains sections of special relevance to the topic of language and culture from a Japanese perspective, especially Language and Culture (pp. 10–29) and Values Which Give Meaning to Facts (pp. 90–110).

Walmsley, J. (1987). *Brit-think, Ameri-think: An irreverent guide to understanding the great cultural ocean that divides us*. New York: Penguin Books. Written by a U.S. American woman married to a man from England, this work provides entertaining explanations of the behaviors of each nationality.

Wolfowitz, C. (1991). *Language style and social space: Stylistic choice in Suriname Javanese*. Champaign: University of Illinois Press. An investigation of links between the stylistic choices in the language of Suriname Javanese speakers and their repertoire of different uses for household space.

Index

This index will help you select activities to suit your purposes. Activities are grouped into four main categories to correspond to the subject matter of Parts II–IV of the text: language-culture, sociolinguistic, culture, and intercultural exploration. Each activity is followed by information about students' language level (beginning [B], intermediate [I], advanced [A]); target audience (children [C], adolescents [AD], adults [A]); duration; and primary skill areas addressed (speaking [S], listening [L], reading [R], writing [W]).

Although the chart highlights aspects of each activity, by level, target audience, and so forth, most activities are adaptable for use in other contexts by making minor modifications.

	Level			Target Audience			Duration	Skill Area(s)			
	B	I	A	C	AD	A		S	L	R	W

Part II: Language-Culture Activities

	B	I	A	C	AD	A	Duration	S	L	R	W
Aba-Zak		•	•		•	•	90 min–2 hrs	•	•		
Culture Exploration	•	•	•		•	•	Variable	•	•		
Artifacts, Sociofacts, Mentifacts	•	•	•		•	•	30 min–1 hr	•	•		•
Fantasy Island	•	•	•	•	•	•	2 hrs +	•	•		
Piglish		•	•		•	•	40–90 min	•	•		
Man From Mars	•	•	•	•	•	•	30 min +	•	•		
The Cocktail Party		•	•		•	•	30 min–1 hr	•	•	•	•
Talking Rocks	•	•	•	•	•	•	2–3 hrs	•	•		

	Target Level			Audience			Duration	Skill Area(s)			
	B	I	A	C	AD	A		S	L	R	W

Part III: Sociolinguistic Activities

	B	I	A	C	AD	A	Duration	S	L	R	W
A Sociocultural Matrix		•	•		•	•	30 min	•	•		
Oops! There I Go Again	•	•	•		•	•	20–30 min	•	•		
What Shall I Call You?		•	•		•	•	1 hr	•	•	•	•
Exploring Relationships		•	•		•	•	30 min–1 hr	•	•	•	•
Choosing (or Avoiding) Topics	•	•	•		•	•	1 hr	•	•	•	
Let Me Talk!			•		•	•	1 hr	•	•		
"Vulgar" Words		•			•	•	40 min	•	•		
What Do You Mean by Polite?			•		•	•	60–90 min	•	•	•	

Part IV: Culture Activities

	B	I	A	C	AD	A	Duration	S	L	R	W
Ethnographic Study	•	•	•		•	•	30 min	•	•	•	•
What's Going On Here?	•	•	•	•	•	•	20–30 min	•	•		
Everyday Tasks	•	•	•	•	•	•	20–30 min	•	•		
Families in Situation Comedies		•	•		•	•	5–6 hrs	•	•		
Home Sweet Home		•	•	•	•	•	6–12 hrs	•	•	•	•
Guess Who's Coming to Visit?		•	•		•	•	1 hr	•	•	•	•
Let's Shop!		•	•		•	•	30–50 min	•	•	•	
In the News		•	•		•	•	30–90 min	•	•	•	•
Exploring Cultural Values		•			•	•	2 x 30 min	•	•	•	•
Exploring Culture		•	•		•	•	30 min–1 hr	•	•	•	•
Room Walk		•	•	•	•	•	1 hr	•	•	•	•
Every Picture/Worth 1,000 Words		•	•	•	•	•	30–45 min	•	•	•	•
Weekly Entertainment Guides	•	•	•		•	•	2 x 1 hr	•	•	•	
Hand(y) Language	•	•	•	•	•	•	15 min	•	•		
Cartoon Culture		•	•	•	•	•	1 hr	•	•		•
Meeyauu!	•	•	•	•	•	•	2–3 hrs	•	•	•	

Also available from TESOL

Books for a Small Planet:
An Multicultural/Intercultural Bibliography
for Young English Language Learners
Dorothy S. Brown

Diversity as Resource:
Redefining Cultural Literacy
Denise E. Murray, Editor

E-mail for English Teaching:
Bringing the Internet and Computer Learning Networks
Into the Language Classroom
Mark Warschauer

More Than a Native Speaker:
An Introduction for Volunteers Teaching Abroad
Don Snow

New Ways in Content-Based Instruction
Donna M. Brinton and Peter Master, Editors

New Ways in Teacher Education
Donald Freeman, with Steve Cornwell, Editors

New Ways in Teaching Adults
Marilyn Lewis, Editor

New Ways in Teaching Young Children
Linda Schinke-Llano and Rebecca Rauff, Editors

New Ways of Using Computers in Language Teaching
Tim Boswood, Editor

New Ways of Using Drama and Literature in Language Teaching
Valerie Whiteson, Editor

Tasks for Independent Language Learning
David Gardner and Lindsay Miller, Editors

For more information, contact
Teachers of English to Speakers of Other Languages, Inc.
1600 Cameron Street, Suite 300
Alexandria, Virginia 22314 USA
Tel 703-836-0774 • Fax 703-836-7864 •
E-mail pubs@tesol.edu • http://www.tesol.edu